05.03.19

Katrina

For your new adventure where you have BOLDLY said yes to Jesus. Keep saying yes & keep living BOLD for Him

XO
Lynds

Endorsements

Rich with the heart-stirring testimony of both the bonds of rebellion and the freedom of obedience, *Live Bold: A Devotional Journal to Strengthen Your Soul* reminds us we aren't in this life alone, encourages us to stop settling for less than the Father promises, and inspires us to thoughtful action that puts Jesus right in the center of it all.

—Tricia Meyer, Ed.D.
Christian school administrator, EE-12

Andrea and Cynthia have crafted a devotional that does more than inspire—it challenges the reader to apply the truth of God's Word to their personal life. This is living bold and precisely the kind of action the world needs to see in these times of global turmoil. Our culture has sought to silence Christians and believes the Christian message is irrelevant. This provides the perfect backdrop for Christians everywhere to demonstrate the transforming power of God's written Word, the Bible, and God's living Word, Jesus Christ. *Live Bold: A Devotional Journal to Strengthen Your Soul* is certain to be a resource God will use to fortify Christians, better enabling them to enjoy the victorious life Christ died to give us, and to present the love and hope this world desperately needs.

—Rev. Pamela Christian
Award-winning author, speaker, media personality, and international minister, host of *Faith To Live By* television series, a ministry of Pamela Christian Ministries www.PamelaChristianMinistries.com.

In a culture where there is an increasing need for truth-based reality, *Live Bold* is a timely devotional for becoming more intentional with our truth. *Live Bold* releases a newfound freedom to explore a deeper connection with God and ourselves, and it also encourages us to not hold back our deepest convictions within our sphere of influence. The authors inspire me to live a more courageous and bold life for Jesus!

—Christine Beitsch-Bahmani
Founding executive director,
CityServe's Compassion Network

All of us experience a world that seems as though it is spinning out of control. As a result, we struggle each day with a sense of powerlessness and vulnerability. The *Live Bold* devotional journal helps us to get our eyes back on the One that can create order out of chaos and hope out of despair. Living bold is about living each day considering Paul's statement, "for God gave us a spirit not of fear but of power and love and self-control" (2 Tim. 1:7 ESV). If you find yourself overwhelmed by the pressures of this world, let the "*Live Bold*" devotional adjust how you frame your life to take risks rather than retreating. The book will remind you "with confidence draw near to the throne of grace, that we may receive mercy and find grace to help in time of need." I highly recommend this weekly devotional. It will lead you to experience new freedom in life.

—Fred Biby
Executive pastor
Bridges Community Church, Fremont, CA

Live Bold

A DEVOTIONAL JOURNAL TO
STRENGTHEN YOUR SOUL

Live Bold

A DEVOTIONAL JOURNAL TO STRENGTHEN YOUR SOUL

ANDREA TOMASSI & CYNTHIA CAVANAUGH

REDEMPTION PRESS

Published by Redemption Press, PO Box 427, Enumclaw, WA 98022

Toll Free (844) 2REDEEM (273-3336)

Redemption Press is honored to present this title in partnership with the author. The views expressed or implied in this work are those of the author. Redemption Press provides our imprint seal representing design excellence, creative content, and high quality production.

Cover Logo Designer: May PL
Website: www.maypldigitalart.etsy.com
Email: maypl1215@gmail.com

Scripture quotations marked (AMP) are taken from the AMPLIFIED® BIBLE. Copyright 1954, 1958, 1962, 1964, 1965, 1987 by The Lockman Foundation. Used by permission.

Scripture quotations marked (ASV) are taken from the American Standard Version. In public domain.

Scripture quotations marked (ESV) are taken from THE HOLY BIBLE, ENGLISH STANDARD VERSION®, Copyright ©2001 by Crossway, a publishing ministry of Good News Publishers. Used by permission.

Scripture quotations marked (GW) are taken from GOD'S WORD®. Copyright ©1995 by God's Word to the Nations. All rights reserved.

Scripture quotations marked (NIV) are taken from THE HOLY BIBLE, NEW INTERNATIONAL VERSION®. Copyright © 1973, 1978 1984, 2011 by Biblica, Inc.™. Used by permission of Zondervan.

Scripture quotations marked (NIRV) are taken from the Holy Bible, NEW INTERNATIONAL READER'S VERSION®. Copyright© 1996, 1998 Biblica. All rights reserved throughout the world. Used by permission of Biblica.

Scripture quotations marked (NLT) are taken from THE HOLY BIBLE, NEW LIVING TRANSLATION, Copyright© 1996, 2004, 2007 by Tyndale House Foundation. Used by permission of Tyndale House Publishers, Inc. Carol Stream, Illinois 60188. All rights reserved. Used by permission.

Scripture quotations marked (TM) are taken from THE MESSAGE: THE BIBLE IN CONTEMPORARY ENGLISH, Copyright© 1993, 1995, 1996, 2000, 2001, 2002. Used by permission of NavPress Publishing Group.

Scripture quotations marked (TV) are taken from THEVOICE™. Copyright© 2008 by Ecclesia Bible Society. Used by permission. All rights reserved.

ISBN 13: 978-1-68314-578-3 (Paperback)

Library of Congress Catalog Card Number: 2018930271

To our grandmother

Mutti

*She lived boldly
and left her grandchildren
a godly legacy.*

Contents

Contents

Introduction

The heart of man plans his way, but the Lord establishes his steps.
—Prov. 16:9 ESV

FAMILY. COUSINS. KINDRED SPIRITS. For as long as we can remember, we have shared the love of all things firstborn. Family history is important to us. Quite by accident we stumbled onto the realization of the need to steward our grandparents' story to live bold and leave a godly legacy.

We learned this past year that our grandmother, Mutti, was a poet. She never published her work, but she had the heart of a writer. We never really thought too much about it until we were together last year speaking at a women's retreat. We were sharing our stories when God put a dream in our hearts. *Rise Up. Write. Together.*

Writing a book is like birthing a baby, and it's hard to do together, and even harder to do when you live in different states. Yet we have discovered that God created us like hand and glove as writers. Our strengths complement each other. We respect one another and aren't threatened by the other's skills or talents. We've camped out at each other's homes for days at a time, shared hotel rooms at conferences, and found a connection to forge a message of influence for our families and others. This is a gift, and we don't take it for granted; we're humbled to carry out the legacy of boldness throughout these pages.

We marvel at how God has orchestrated every detail of our lives, and we're grateful to share this *Live Bold* devotional with you. In it, we've both shared our stories of discovering what it means to live bold. Yes, we are still a work in process. Our prayer is that you will not only be encouraged, but radically influenced to love Jesus, so you too can walk boldly in Christ.

Andrea & Cynthia

CHAPTER ONE

Bold Faith

INTRODUCTION
THE POWER OF FAITH

Cynthia

FAITH IS THE POWER to see what you can't see.

Faith is the movement in life that propels us to take risks, to trust, to believe.

Faith, as Jesus said, needs only to be as small as a mustard seed to be active.

It is the beginning, the start, and the force that overcomes our inertia and pushes us into the unknown.

It is what fuels our hope when all seems hopeless.

Faith believes when impossible circumstances dictate otherwise.

Does your faith feel weak and small at this moment? Let me reassure you that those feelings are normal and human.

What is not normal is "bold faith" that unleashes the supernatural power we are promised. We have full access to the same power that raised Jesus from the dead. Paul says, "I also pray that you will understand the incredible greatness of God's power for us who believe him. This is the same mighty power that raised Christ from the dead and seated him in the place of honor at God's right hand in the heavenly realms" (Eph. 1:19–20 NLT).

This "same" power gives us confidence to be bold in our faith. It takes guts to have bold faith, especially when the scene in front of us is foggy and unclear.

Let me offer some questions for reflection as we begin this devotional journey.

- Where is your faith at today?
- Can you believe God is offering you the "same" power he granted to his Son when Jesus walked away from the tomb?
- Can you believe God for your impossible circumstance?
- Can you muster up a seed of faith and give it back to God, asking him to help you grow?

This month our prayer is that you can embrace bold faith in your everyday life. Be prepared. Watch out. Your bold faith isn't hidden; it's in plain sight because God won't hide himself from you when you need him most. It might feel as if he is far away, but he is right next to you offering you his help.

Grasp your faith tight and hold on to believe.

This is the beauty of our faith—with God everything is possible to live boldly with godly confidence.

BOLD FAITH - Week One
CAN YOU TRUST GOD?

Andrea

It took me thirty minutes to push *Send.* Just a few months earlier, I sat down my two adult children and my youngest, who was still in high school at the time, to tell them I had filed divorce papers. It was one of the hardest things I have ever had to do. Their father and I had been separated for six months and, through my eyes, our future looked hopeless. I became impatient with God and decided to take matters into my own hands.

Now fast-forward two months. As I sat in my car and typed out an email to my attorney, I heard God clearer than ever before: "Andrea, do you trust me?" My finger stayed on the send button for what seemed like forever. I was taking the *boldest* step I had ever taken. I was calling off the divorce.

During the previous two months, the Holy Spirit had touched me deeply. All I could hear was, "You don't see what I see . . . *stop!*"

What will everyone think of me? I thought. I was confused. I truly thought I heard God clearly telling me to proceed. I never would have involved my children if I wasn't completely sure.

But I was fooled. "And no wonder, for Satan himself masquerades as an angel of light" (2 Cor. 11:14 NIV).

Then I did it! I hit send and gave my attorney the same instructions God had given me. *Call it off and give it away! Don't fight; I will take care of you.*

So I did. I told my attorney my husband could have the business, the house, everything, and he could give me what he felt was fair. Now,

I know some of you reading this right now probably think I was a bit crazy. Trust me, you aren't the only ones.

But I knew fighting about money and material things would rip our family apart. God promised he would take care of me, so I closed my eyes and pushed *Send*.

How does this story end? Just like he said he would. On my birthday, three years ago, my husband handed me my wedding ring back and asked me, "Do you want to do this all over again with me?"

Hello? Yes. Of course. I thought you'd never ask.

God gave me the desires of my heart just as he promised. He is faithful, my friends; he is so faithful!

BOLD ACTION STEP

Get quiet with God this week and ask him to show you where your faith needs some work. In what area of your life do you need to step out *boldly in faith*?

 ### VERSE OF THE WEEK

At that same time, I begged God: "God, my Master, you let me in on the beginnings, you let me see your greatness, you let me see your might—what god in Heaven or Earth can do anything like what you've done!"

(Deut. 3:23–24 MSG)

⚓ MY BOLD THOUGHTS

. . . .

. . . .

. . . .

. . . .

. . . .

. . . .

. . . .

. . . .

. . . .

. . . .

. . . .

. . . .

BOLD FAITH - Week Two
FAITH IN HARD TIMES

Cynthia

I sat in the surgical waiting room waiting for news about my dad. As hour after hour passed, I watched people waiting, some chatting quietly, others watching mindless shows on TV. The doctors would come searching for a patient's family and take them into the hallway to deliver their news either good or bad. It was sobering to say the least.

When our turn came, we received good news but still had to wait for the pathology report. A few days later, on the plane ride home, I couldn't stand the wait any longer. I bought thirty minutes of Wi-Fi to tap into the outside world. A text came saying, "100 percent clean, no cancer, no further treatment."

I cried. This wasn't what the surgeon had told us at first.

My dad told me about the day of his surgery. He said, "I woke up feeling an overwhelming presence like God was right next to me, reassuring me I would be okay, he cautiously shared, "You might find that weird."

"Of course not!" I said. God can reveal himself in any way he chooses, even giving us a tangible physical sense of his closeness when we are afraid.

I realize not everyone gets this kind of report after waiting and pounding the doors of heaven. God always answers, but maybe not in the way we hope for. This time he spared my dad from further surgery and treatment.

I've heard people say, "God is so faithful and so good to have answered." Now *that* sounds weird to me! God doesn't change; he is always good and always faithful, even when the outcome isn't what we hope for.

My dad has a pure faith. Because of Dad's faithfulness, I believe God chose to reveal himself to Dad because he truly asked for it, even with shaky faith. In 2 Samuel 22:26 (NIV) we read, "To the faithful you show yourself faithful, to the blameless you show yourself blameless." Either way, no matter the outcome, my dad knew that he was not alone.

Can I remind you that you, too, are not alone? Thankfully, God's faithfulness isn't dependent on our faith. He knows we are frail. He knows it's hard to hang on when life gets hard.

Today I encourage you to make a choice to trust with bold faith and believe, "The word of the Lord is right and true; he is faithful in all he does" (Ps. 33:4 NIV).

 BOLD ACTION STEP

In what part of your life are you struggling to believe God? Write it down and present it back to him with a whispered prayer of "God, I need your help." Every day this week read your prayer out loud as a declaration to start your day.

 VERSE OF THE WEEK

For the word of the Lord holds true, and we can trust everything he does.

(Ps. 33:4 NLT)

MY BOLD THOUGHTS

BOLD FAITH - Week Three
CHOOSING TO BELIEVE

Andrea

I recently spent a week at my cousin Cynthia's home for a mini writing retreat. As always, there were fresh towels and welcome gifts that included some sort of chocolate. A few days into my trip, I started my morning routine a bit earlier, wanting to get a head start on my day.

I brushed my teeth and washed my face, but as I grabbed for the towel, I realized it wasn't there. With my eyes still closed and water dripping from my face, I remembered the towel was hanging over the shower. I turned around with my eyes still closed and walked toward the shower with my arms stretched out in front of me like a mummy. If I continued walking in that general direction, I knew my hands would eventually meet the towel. I had faith the towel was there because I knew I put it there the morning before.

Having faith means walking towards something, not because you necessarily see it, but because you know it's there.

It's choosing to believe in things when common sense tells you not to.

Each time God comes through and reveals his faithfulness, we grow a more profound faith. This builds *bold* faith to believe the next time we doubt if God is still there.

When Jesus appeared to his disciples after his resurrection, Thomas, one of the Twelve, wasn't with them. When the other disciples told him they had seen Jesus, he doubted and said, "Unless I see the nail marks in his hands and put my finger where the nails were, and put my hand into his side, I will not believe" (John 20:25 NIV).

A week later Jesus came and stood among the Twelve again. He told Thomas to look at his hands, to stop doubting, and to believe. Suddenly,

Thomas believed because he saw with his own eyes. He yelled, "My Lord and my God!" Just then, Jesus said to him, "Because you have seen me, you have believed; blessed are those who have not seen and yet have believed" (John 20:29 NIV).

How favored are those who believe without seeing?

When was the last time you had this kind of faith?

We don't know what the future holds; we are unaware of the impending darkness, but because of our faith, we can continue searching for the light.

 BOLD ACTION STEP

What are you contemplating doing this week that could grow your faith? Is there something you've been hesitant about because you're choosing to believe with your eyes instead of your heart?

 VERSE OF THE WEEK

Blessed is she who has believed that the Lord would fulfill his promises to her!

(Luke 1:45 NIV)

MY BOLD THOUGHTS

BOLD FAITH - Week Four
FAITH FOR THE NEXT STEP

Cynthia

When the grandkids come to spend the night, we have a routine before we put them to bed. Their jammies go on and they brush their teeth with anticipation of being able to read in bed by flashlight. I tuck them in, sing, pray, and turn out the lights. They eagerly turn on their flashlights and begin their stack of books they've chosen for the night. Once in awhile I love to linger at the door and watch them. And though they can't see anything else in the room, they have just enough light to read. They trust in the little beam of light even though it is black around them. By faith in the light they read.

Isn't that just like our faith? When we take a step of faith, God gives us just enough light to see where to place our next step. We can walk boldly ahead without stumbling.

When I read the faith chapter—Hebrews 11—I am reassured we are not alone on this journey of faith.

> By faith we understand God as the creator.
> By faith Abel offered his sacrifice.
> By faith Enoch was taken to heaven.
> By faith Noah built the ark.
> By faith Abraham obeyed and went to a new land.
> By faith Sarah conceived a son.
> By faith Isaac gave a blessing to his future descendants.
> By faith Jacob blessed his grandchildren in Egypt.
> By faith Moses was hidden as a baby .
> By faith the Israelites crossed the Red Sea.

By faith the walls of Jericho fell.

By faith Rahab hid the spies and her life was spared when Jericho fell.

By faith we believe and receive Jesus' death and resurrection, trusting we will spend eternity with him forever.

It is by faith we receive all God has planned and prepared for us. By faith we trust he knows our future. By faith we pray. By faith we forgive. By faith we love. And by faith we wake up each day and ask for his help to walk boldly.

 **BOLD ACTION STEP**

Write your personal "by faith" chapter this week. Each day add at least two *by faith* statements. At the end of the week pray over it and ask God to increase your faith to believe him.

 VERSE OF THE WEEK

Faith shows the reality of what we hope for; it is the evidence of things we cannot see.

(Heb. 11:1 NLT)

MY BOLD THOUGHTS

. . . .

. . . .

. . . .

. . . .

. . . .

. . . .

. . . .

. . . .

. . . .

. . . .

. . . .

BOLD FAITH - Week Five
TAKING A LEAP OF FAITH

Andrea

When we decide to step out of our comfort zone and take a leap of faith, miracles happen.

What exactly is a *leap of faith*? Let's break it down, shall we? *Leap* is defined as "to jump or spring a long way, to a great height." And *faith* means "complete trust or confidence in someone or something."

Here's my perspective on taking a leap of faith. To me, a leap of faith is when we're all in, acting out of obedience with complete trust and confidence because of the promise God has placed in our hearts.

I love to write. It's been a steady promise in my heart. I'd taken a creative writing class in high school, and always had a passion for writing poetry, most recently for writing songs. As I continued writing, the words *One day you will write a book* flooded my mind.

As the years went on, that little spark began to ignite until it overwhelmed my heart. I knew it was a promise. I patiently waited for my "one day."

Others may not share the same level of faith we do; they may not be on the same page. Some people may choose to be part of the process, run alongside us, and cheer us on. Some may just sit back and watch it all unfold from the sidelines. Others may not ever show up to the race.

But don't be discouraged, sweet friend. God is just waiting to see how faithful we are with the things he has called us to do. God sees your heart. He knows how deeply you desire to please him. As long as your actions stem from the right motives, you can trust you will be richly blessed.

BOLD ACTION STEP

Is there an area of your life in which you need to take a leap of faith? Has God put a promise in your heart? What is holding you back from leaping?

 VERSE OF THE WEEK

So let God work his will in you. Yell a loud *no* to the Devil and watch him scamper. Say a quiet *yes* to God and he'll be there in no time. Quit dabbling in sin. Purify your inner life. Quit playing the field. Hit bottom, and cry your eyes out. The fun and games are over. Get serious, really serious. Get down on your knees before the Master; it's the only way you'll get on your feet.

(James 4:8–10 MSG)

MY BOLD THOUGHTS

CHAPTER TWO

Bold Obedience

INTRODUCTION
THE OBEDIENCE CONNECTION

Andrea

THINK BACK TO WHEN you were young. Wouldn't you agree your household was much more pleasant when you followed your parents' directions? Things tend to run smoother when everyone is getting along—like when our kids get their homework done without being asked. Let the angels sing "Hallelujah" when you see your son cleaning out his room after three months of nagging. It's time for the "happy dance!"

Now let's look at a different scenario. Your daughter is on the Internet against your wishes instead of doing her homework, and she hasn't touched her chores. I'm sure you see where I'm going with this. This scenario results in a stressful home that can leave parents feeling disconnected and far away from their kids.

It's no different with God. Closeness to God isn't a feeling, but rather it comes from acts of obedience.

Friends, God is our heavenly Father, and we are his precious children. When he asks us to be obedient, it often requires taking a bold step. When we are disobedient, it can leave us feeling disconnected, and we wonder why we can't hear God.

It's like talking to a friend on your cell phone when suddenly your call gets disconnected right in the middle of the conversation. It's happened to me, and I've continued talking for several minutes without even knowing the call had been dropped. After finally noticing the silence on the other end, I realized I had been talking, but nobody was listening.

I've found the more I walk in line with God's will, the closer I feel to him. It is my prayer this week that you can find time to get "reconnected" with Jesus. Don't miss your message because of a bad connection.

BOLD OBEDIENCE - Week 6
DIRTY OVENS AND CRUSTY HEARTS

Cynthia

I have a confession. I haven't cleaned the inside of my oven since we moved into our house. Please don't judge me. I hadn't thought it looked too dirty until it was sparkly clean.

As I was wiping out the charcoal dust I noticed some extra-stubborn baked-on spots that needed a little soft scrub and muscle.

God gave me a picture of my own heart. There are crevices that are months and probably years old that I have turned on the self-cleaning button on thinking that it was fine.

I wasn't obedient.

He reminded me I need to get a little "Holy Spirit Soft Scrub" and put some muscle into those stubborn spots of bad habits and wrong thinking patterns.

I realized that those wrong thinking patterns represented a few crusty baked-on places in my heart. When life throws me some curveballs and I can't fix any of it, it's frustrating! The negative thoughts pile on one another. They can build and build until they scream for my attention.

I am choosing to be obedient to stop long enough to pay attention to the crusty places and what needs to be surrendered in my heart. This process may take longer than it took for me to clean my oven.

Try these steps to loosen the gunk on a baked-on crusty heart.

- Stop. Step back and pay attention; listen to that still small voice.
- Confess. Be honest with yourself and God. We may think God doesn't know about the crusty, baked-on places in our hearts. He does! And the beautiful part is he still loves us no matter how thick or crusty those layers might be.
- Scrub and then scrub some more. Make time to reflect. Then use the tools God has given us to scour those places away by renewing our minds with his promises.

Scrubbing the baked-on crusty junk in my oven was hard. My shoulder hurt from pressing in.

It's the same way when we work at being obedient to rid ourselves of old habits—it can hurt and it might take a while.

After King David sinned and repented, he wrote this: "Create a clean heart in me, O God, and renew a faithful spirit within me" (Ps. 51:10 GW).

After I've been obedient and the crusty places are removed, I'm asking God to clean me up, create new thoughts in me, and renew in me a faithful spirit.

How about you?

 BOLD ACTION STEP

What crusty baked-on places are layering up in your heart? Take a few moments to stop, confess, and scrub.

 VERSE OF THE WEEK

Create a clean heart in me, O God, and renew a faithful spirit within me.

(Ps. 51:10 GW)

⚓ MY BOLD THOUGHTS

· ·

· ·

· ·

· ·

· ·

· ·

· ·

· ·

· ·

· ·

· ·

BOLD OBEDIENCE - Week 7
WRITTEN IN PENCIL

Andrea

Do you sometimes wonder why bad things happen, often to the best of people? It is a difficult question, especially when God asks you step out in bold obedience. Our minds are not even capable of understanding.

Let me share a story with you that I've told to each of my children since they were small.

One day, God opened a book named _____ (insert your name here). This wasn't just any book; this was your special book with no other like it. God grabbed a pencil like the short little pencils without erasers used to keep score when playing miniature golf, or the ones you see filling the holes in church pews on Sunday mornings. He meticulously lined each page carefully with chosen gifts and blessings any loving father would give to his children.

Take a minute to pause and imagine what's written in your book. Could it be filled with all your hopes and dreams and the desires of your heart?

Sadly, you will never know everything that is written.

Do you know why God uses a pencil? It's because the words he has written were never meant to be changed. Our Father has written the perfect version of your life according to his will. Can you imagine anything more perfect?

Unfortunately, a pencil isn't the only tool he uses. When God picks up a marker, a sense of sadness flashes across his face because he knows the marker is permanent. It's simple. Each time you make decisions based on your will and not his, he uses a marker to write in your story, replacing the plans he originally intended for you. The soft gray hue of lead is now hidden underneath dark ink, bleeding through the pages that follow.

There is a lesson to be learned with every choice we make, but since God extends grace, we are always offered a second chance to get it right. Sadly, I know I will never know everything God has written in my book—at least not on this side of heaven.

I can ask the Holy Spirit to lead me to make good choices by including him in my decisions.

Next time you see a pencil without an eraser, remember God is writing your story. Don't miss his best plans for your life.

 BOLD ACTION STEP

Would you be more mindful about the decision you make if you knew you'd receive God's very best? What decision do you need to bring before God today? Ask him to give you discernment so you can be in line with his will for your life.

 VERSE OF THE WEEK

For I know the plans I have for you, declares the Lord, plans for welfare and not for evil, to give you a future and a hope.

(Jer. 29:11 ESV)

⚓ MY BOLD THOUGHTS

. . . .

. . . .

. . . .

. . . .

. . . .

. . . .

. . . .

. . . .

. . . .

. . . .

. . . .

. . . .

BOLD OBEDIENCE - Week 8
KNEES DOWN AND HANDS UP

Cynthia

I was trying to merge onto the freeway recently when a semi-truck apparently couldn't see me and nearly ran me off the road. I took the opportunity to let him know how rude I thought he was. Then I realized he might not have seen my car. After all, it was my responsibility to yield to the traffic.

Yielding can be difficult when there is an obstacle in the way—and I am not talking about driving. When there are roadblocks in life they can stop us in our tracks and scream to us to give up. It's easier to play it safe and give up instead of plowing through and persevering. That's where the hard work of obedience comes into play. When we yield to God in spite of the obstacle, we are obedient.

I once heard a speaker say, "Yielding means knees down and hands up." Not exactly the position I naturally move to. Why is it that we tend to think that obedience should be easy or that God should remove the obstacles before we can be obedient? Wouldn't that be much easier? If you've been a Christ follower for a while, you know that easy isn't always the best path to growth.

These are some steps I've learned to yield and lean toward obedience.

#1 Change my attitude – Stop whining and complaining and lean in. Philippians 2:5 talks about having the mind of Christ. He is the example.

He had a lot to complain and whine about and yet he was obedient, "becoming obedient to the point of death" (Philippians 2:8 ESV).

#2 Change my perspective – Learn to embrace the humility of the situation and ask God how to look at the obstacle differently. Don't allow lock down and lock in to see the obstacle from one perspective.

#3 Change the challenge – instead of fighting the obstacle trying to push it out of the way, look for new ways to adapt to the roadblock so you can continue to move forward. Don't fight the obstacle—yield!

Once I took responsibility to consider the truck driver and not curse him for being the obstacle, I was able to safely yield onto the freeway. This is also true when we obey and surrender the obstacles in our lives to God and yield to his will.

BOLD ACTION STEP

Where are you frustrated right now? Name the obstacle you might be fighting, and choose to yield to God in obedience. Write a prayer making a choice to yield in obedience.

 VERSE OF THE WEEK

Stay alert! I am God, the God of everything living. Is there anything I can't do?

(Jer. 32:27 MSG)

⚓ MY BOLD THOUGHTS

· ·

· ·

· ·

· ·

· ·

· ·

· ·

· ·

· ·

· ·

· ·

BOLD OBEDIENCE - Week 9
WAIT FOR THE PROMISE

Andrea

Remember how I told you about the promise God put in my heart that I would write? Well, there were eight long years in between the promise and the fulfillment. When I'd have an intense desire to document situations, conversations, and milestones that were significant markers in my life, each time I'd sense a still, sweet voice whispering, *Write that down; you're going to need that one day.* I never quite understood the meaning behind it, but I knew it was a journey of obedience. I knew one day God would show me in his time.

When the incredible opportunity presented itself to write this book with my cousin Cynthia, I knew it was what God had promised so long ago. I downloaded all my notes from my phone to my laptop, and surprisingly, there were over 630 of them. Many of them are the words you are reading on these pages.

I have learned you don't always need to understand, you don't need to agree, and you don't even need to believe it—but the one thing we do need to do is obey.

Rebekah in the Old Testament agreed to leave her family and travel to marry Isaac, a man she had never met, because she knew this was God's will. When she did not conceive after twenty years, Isaac prayed for his wife and she had twin sons, Esau and Jacob. God blessed Rebekah because of her obedience. Blessings always follow obedience. They may not come right away; it might be one year, ten years, or twenty years later, as with Rebekah, buy they will come.

This past Christmas my two adult sons and daughter put a large check in my Christmas stocking. The card made me cry. It read:

> You've always believed in our hopes and dreams; now it's time for us to do that for you. You have showed us that no matter what age or circumstances in life, it is never too late to chase your dreams. We want you to know we support you and believe in you and the gift and wisdom God has blessed you with. We would like to cover your schooling for the next semester because you deserve it.

When my daughter told me how all this came about, she wiped the tears from her own face. "I wasn't sure how I was going to come up with the money," she said, "but I knew this was something God wanted me to do." When she opened two Christmas cards earlier that day, in them was enough money to cover her share of the gift, with a few hundred dollars left over. "Mom," she said, "God gave back to me because I was obedient for you!"

Proud mom. Awesome kids. Amazing God!

 BOLD ACTION STEP

Read Genesis 24, 25:19–26 and ask God to show you how you can have the same kind of willing obedience as Rebekah. Write down what's on your heart today.

 VERSE OF THE WEEK

I will surely bless you and make your descendants as numerous as the stars in the sky and as the sand on the seashore. Your descendants will take possession of the cities of their enemies, and through your offspring all nations on earth will be blessed, because you have obeyed me.

(Gen. 22:17–18 NIV)

MY BOLD THOUGHTS

CHAPTER THREE

Bold Identity

INTRODUCTION
IDENTITY CRISIS

Cynthia

MY FATHER HAS AFFECTIONATELY called me his Cinderella for as long as I can remember. My story, unlike that of the fairy-tale Cinderella, is not the tale of a servant girl living happily ever after with her prince. Rather, it is a tale of a woman experiencing brokenness, understanding redemption, and knowing what it means to walk out what that word means every day of my life.

Part of my understanding of redemption is what you might call my coming of a mature spiritual age. I don't do it perfectly. It's like Paul said: "Not that I have already obtained all this, or have already arrived at my goal, but I press on to take hold of that for which Christ Jesus took hold of me" (Phil. 3:12 NIV). This is my identity.

In a world where we often identify ourselves by what we do, who we are, what we own, and what we say, there is only one place our identity can be entirely secure—in Jesus Christ. God's love story to the world is a story of sacrificial love. We are the beneficiaries of redemption to repair our broken identity. When we understand the truth of redemption, we can embrace our identity. We no longer need to chase after success and perform to be accepted, loved, and cherished, because we already are accepted, loved, and cherished in Christ.

As we look at identity in this chapter, I pray that stepping out in bold faith will empower you to embrace a new bold identity rooted in the truth of redemption.

BOLD IDENTITY - Week 10
THE FINAL WORD

Andrea

If God had a refrigerator, your picture would be on it!

Our value isn't based on what we've done, and it most certainly is not defined by who you know. Nor is it based on what we do for a living or the clothes we wear, what people say about us, our choices, or our performances.

Our value is defined by the simple fact that we are children of God. We don't have to do anything. God will never love us more than he does right this very moment. His love for us is the same love he had the day his one and only Son was nailed to a cross.

Sadly, sometimes even the people closest to you can be among those who won't ever see your greatness. The problem is, they're looking at you through a lens of expectation. They base their opinions from their perspectives and not in who God created you to be. Often, their views have nothing to do with you, but rather come from their brokenness and past hurt.

Some may not be able to acknowledge your gifts or talents. But friend, God sees your gifts. He's the one who blessed you with them in the first place.

I've lived most of my life with the need for other people's approval; I defined my identity around it.

Recently, I've realized that I should be more concerned with what God thinks of me than what everyone else thinks of me. I've been asking myself:

"Am I using the gifts God has given me for his glory?"

"Are my actions matching what I speak?"

These are the things I should be focusing my energy on. Don't get me wrong. Everyone is entitled to their own opinions, and I believe constructive criticism is essential to personal growth. But before we believe what others say as gospel truth, wwe need to open our Bibles, meditate on God's Word, and ask ourselves, "Is that what God says about me?"

How about asking a trusted friend if she sees you the same way? We shouldn't take what others say to be the *final* word. Only God has the final word, and he says you are holy and blameless in his sight.

BOLD ACTION STEP

Who does God say you are? Write down your favorite verses that define you in Christ. Meditate on them this week.

 VERSE OF THE WEEK

Even before he made the world, God loved us and chose us in Christ to be holy and without fault in his eyes.

(Eph. 1:4 NLT)

MY BOLD THOUGHTS

BOLD IDENTITY - Week 11
AMBASSADORS OF LOVE

Cynthia

It's been hard not to jump in and join the rants and raves on social media with what's been happening in our country and around the world. I've read and listened, watched and prayed on what seems to have imploded. It makes me sick and sad all at the same time and I wonder, just wonder, what God sees when he watches.

Within the noise and madness of our world, God is in the process of redeeming all of us. It signifies just how patient he really is. I struggle with God's patience at times, and yet I know it is a part of his redemptive narrative.

Can we in our bantering back and forth choose to state our opinions carefully, yet with courage, and let them be sprinkled with kindness?

I believe we can when we know who we are and whom we belong to.

When our identity is secure in the King of heaven, we can separate for a moment and filter our opinions through a different perspective. Our rants become kinder, our words are softer, and grace colors our life.

Why? Because when we know where we belong and who holds our future, our identity isn't threatened. We don't have anything to prove. We don't have to get ramped up to make our point. Our identity rests in the sovereign God of the universe. We can be ambassadors of reconciliation and love.

There is a line in the recent remake of *Cinderella* at the end of the story when the prince discovers his mystery princess and asks, "Who are you?"

She steps forward and says, "I am Cinderella. I'm no princess. I have no carriage, no parents, no dowry, and I don't even know if that beautiful slipper will fit. But if it does, will you take me as I am?"

And I see myself presenting myself to the ruler of heaven, asking the same question: "Will you take me as I am?"

To which he whispers: You are my treasure (Ex. 19:5), I rejoice over you with singing (Zeph. 3:17), as a shepherd carries a lamb, I have carried you close to my heart (Isa. 40:11). One day I will wipe away every tear from your eyes (Rev. 21:3–4).

This is the redemption God longs to give to us through his So,n Jesus, as we present ourselves with all our flaws and failings. This is our strong identity.

 BOLD ACTION STEP

This next week try to refrain from responding to a rant you read on social media. Choose instead to listen and pray.

 VERSE OF THE WEEK

He will tend his flock like a shepherd; he will gather the lambs in his arms; he will carry them in his bosom, and gently lead those that are with young.

(Isa. 40:11 ESV)

⚓ MY BOLD THOUGHTS

. . . .

. . . .

. . . .

. . . .

. . . .

. . . .

. . . .

. . . .

. . . .

. . . .

. . . .

. . . .

BOLD IDENTITY - Week 12
WHO AM I?

Andrea

When I was a teenager, I lived a double life. Very involved with the youth group at my church, I also sang on the worship team and helped my mom with the Awana program. When I was around friends at school, I followed what they were doing, although I knew I shouldn't. The need to fit in took precedence over my morals.

As I got older, this turned into codependence, and I did things because I wanted people to like me. After working a full-time job and taking care of my young children, I'd stay up all hours of the night cleaning the house so my husband would be happy.

As women, we can get caught up in our identities being defined by what we do, instead of being found in Jesus. We take on the roles of wives, mothers, caregivers, business owners, teachers, carpool drivers, and the list goes on and on. I'm sure you could add to the list with a few of your own.

There comes a time in most of our lives when we have this deep-seated need to discover who we are. Somewhere in between the many roles we've played over the years, pieces of us lie scattered along the journey.

Although I think self-discovery is important, we need to place more emphasis on the importance of "whose" we are rather than "who" we are.

I know I have been born into the family of God—much like being part of a well-known prestigious family. I have a right to an inheritance for no other reason than because of who my Father is.

He is the King of kings. The Lord of lords. So that makes me royalty! I am a daughter of the King. That's who I am.

I know apart from Jesus Christ, I am nothing. And that brings me to the battle. We are in a constant battle, my friends.

You can't fight an enemy if you don't know his name. So, name him. Satan is his name and destroying you is his game. He wants nothing more than to change the way you see yourself. He knows God holds the victory in the end.

The only thing he can control is our minds. We decide how long we entertain those negative thoughts. I once thought surrender was a one-way ticket, a one-time thing. Boy, was I wrong! We need to surrender our minds every morning, so when we look in the mirror, we see more of Christ and less of us.

 BOLD ACTION STEP

Write out a prayer to God to pray each morning over the next week (and daily in the future). Include statements of your identity and the truth of whose you are. He already knows, but he's waiting for you to *claim* it, *believe* it, and *own* it.

VERSE OF THE WEEK

But to all who did receive him, who believed in his name, he gave the right to become children of God.

(John 1:12 ESV)

MY BOLD THOUGHTS

. . . .

. . . .

. . . .

. . . .

. . . .

. . . .

. . . .

. . . .

. . . .

. . . .

. . . .

. . . .

BOLD IDENTITY - Week 13
IDENTITY UNDER ATTACK

Cynthia

"Somebody is using our identity!" When my husband Kevin and I found out our personal information had been compromised, it was a terrible feeling. Since this has happened more than once, we now have our identity monitored so our personal information stays secure.

It's no secret that identity theft is on the rise. Every day our information is potentially threatened in the online world.

But another type of identity under attack is our understanding of our personal identity—who God created us to be.

In the university classroom where I teach, the students are international students working toward a leadership degree. One of the key topics I communicate is how to lead from a base of embracing their unique identities. I tell them strong, successful leaders have a secure identity that in turn allows them to lead with godly characteristics such as humility, authenticity, and integrity.

When we understand who we are from God's perspective, our desperate need to prove ourselves is removed.

Isolation is one of the detractors that keeps us from embracing a secure identity. We isolate when we feel insecure about who we are.

The enemy's strategy is to keep us separated from God so we won't understand that a sure identity lies in who he created us to be, and how we are reflections of God's image. Satan is an identity thief. When our identity isn't secure in Jesus Christ, we get deterred from taking the initiative for our own lives, and that keeps us from taking action. We miss God's purpose and plan for our lives as we wander aimlessly. We try on all sorts of identities, but we miss the very significant identity God has blessed us with.

I've struggled with this. For much of my life I tried to wear an identity that wasn't created for me.

The solution to embracing my personal identity has been to study the character of God and understand more deeply who *he* is. As I've done this, an anchor has dropped down securely in my soul. I have embraced the image of God in my own life, and that has set me free from the trap of the lies I believed for so long.

 BOLD ACTION STEP

How about you? What identity have you been wearing that isn't yours? What have you allowed Satan to steal from you? Pull out your Bible and choose ten verses on the character of God. Write a declaration alongside these verses of who God is. Then write your own identity statement reflecting God's image in your life.

 VERSE OF THE WEEK

For we are his workmanship, created in Christ Jesus for good works, which God prepared beforehand, that we should walk in them.

(Eph. 2:10 ESV)

⚓ MY BOLD THOUGHTS

. . . .

. . . .

. . . .

. . . .

. . . .

. . . .

. . . .

. . . .

. . . .

. . . .

. . . .

CHAPTER FOUR

Bold Love and Forgiveness

INTRODUCTION
CHOOSE TO FORGIVE

Andrea
IT'S NOT ALWAYS EASY to do the right thing.

There are times when we need to do the right thing for no other reason other than it's the right thing to do. "But even if you should suffer for what is right, you are blessed" (1 Peter 3:14a NIV). When we live our lives like that, situations have a way of working themselves out.

God is the author of our stories and the director of our lives.

During seasons of pain in my life, I've held on to this verse, and I'd like to share it with you. "And we know that for those who love God all things work together for good, for those who are called according to his purpose" (Rom. 8:28 ESV).

We've all experienced pain—from death to betrayal, heartbreak, sadness, abandonment, abuse, disappointment, physical pain, and discouragement. Trust me when I tell you there is a purpose for our pain.

Sometimes the hardest thing to do is forgive someone who we feel does not deserve our forgiveness. Matthew 6:14 (NIV) says, "For if you forgive other people when they sin against you, your heavenly Father will also forgive you."

Do you believe that? You see, we can't just choose to believe the things in the Bible that seem easy. We also need to believe the hard things. We need to believe all of it!

It's a choice. Will you choose this week to believe God's Word? God can be trusted to work *everything* in our lives for our good.

BOLD LOVE AND BOLD FORGIVENESS - Week 14
PURSUING LOVE

Cynthia

One summer when our boys were small, Kevin and I ministered together at a family camp in Montana. We were taking a short break after lunch, and our three boys were playing together with friends—or so we thought. Jordan, our three-year-old middle son, suddenly went MIA, aka missing in action. At first, we weren't too concerned, because he was known to be an escape artist. We were sure he was just around the corner with friends. One of those friends, a resident camper, was quite a bit older and had a reputation of disappearing across the road to the raging river. Now he was missing too. After a brief search, we couldn't find either of them anywhere.

A few hours later as we were frantic with worry and desperation, we saw Jordan sauntering happily across the field toward us. Every available adult had been searching the perimeter of the camp, including the riverfront, for the missing boys. Where had Jordan been all this time? He and a new little girlfriend had been brushing their teeth and playing games in an RV, oblivious that his parents were looking for him.

As I grabbed him and held him tight, I cried tears of relief. Scared, he said sweetly, "Mommy, what's wrong?" Jordan was unaware he was missing.

Isn't that just like us? We think we *found* Jesus, but he pursues us with his love. And isn't that just like God? He doesn't give up. He doesn't relent. He will do anything to draw us to himself, because he can do no less as the author of redeeming love.

Just like my son Jordan, we don't even know how lost we are, and God still pursues us.

The parable of the lost sheep in Luke 15:1–7 emphasizes the "joy in heaven over one sinner who repents." God's love and forgiveness extends to all of us who are lost—from the moment we take a step to surrender to Jesus and each time we stray. God continues to woo us to himself—not to control us, but because he loves us like the lost lamb in the story of Luke. We are important to him, and nothing can separate us from his love.

BOLD ACTION STEP

Read the story about the lost sheep in Luke 15:1–7. When did you first realize you were lost? How did Jesus find you? Write a thank-you note to God, telling him how grateful you are for his relentless love that pursues you.

 VERSE OF THE WEEK

And I am convinced that nothing can ever separate us from God's love. Neither death nor life, neither angels nor demons, neither our fears for today nor our worries about tomorrow—not even the powers of hell can separate us from God's love.

(Rom. 8:38 NLT)

⚓ MY BOLD THOUGHTS

BOLD LOVE AND FORGIVENESS - Week 15
NOW YOU SEE IT, NOW YOU DON'T

Andrea

I have been blessed to live at the top of the hill with amazing views of both sunrises and sunsets. My husband and I took a leap of faith and signed the papers on our house while we were legally separated. We both took this faith step together because we trusted God would fix our hearts.

One morning I looked out at the reflection of the sun over twenty miles away on windows across San Francisco Bay. From where I was standing, I couldn't see the sun, but only gray, dark clouds.

I thought about how easily we get caught up in the doom and gloom of a situation and miss the lesson. That morning I was reminded the sun always shines, whether we see it or not.

Have you ever taken off in a plane in the middle of a storm? You might have experienced a little turbulence as the plane ascended to the required altitude. Once the plane broke through the final cloud, there was nothing but sunshine and pillows of clouds.

Just last week I was driving in a downpour and could see nothing but rain clouds. Suddenly, the clouds disappeared, revealing clear, baby-blue sunny skies. That was a reminder to stop dwelling on the negative things in my life and start loving on the people God has entrusted me with.

Things aren't always the way they seem, but God knows what he's doing. And he most certainly doesn't need any help from us! God's job is to judge, the Holy Spirit's job is to convict, and our job is to *love*! "The Lord will fight for you, and you have only to be silent," says Exodus 14:14 (ESV). He's here and ready to fight! The light of the Son is upon us, even when we have moments when we are surrounded by dark clouds and feel hopeless.

BOLD ACTION STEP

Remember, God is always fighting for you. Journal your thoughts this week as God reminds you he will never stop fighting for you.

 VERSE OF THE WEEK

Some of you wandered for years in the desert, looking but not finding a good place to live, half-starved and parched with thirst, staggering and stumbling, on the brink of exhaustion. Then, in your desperate condition, you called out to God. He got you out in the nick of time; he put your feet on a wonderful road that took you straight to a good place to live. So thank God for his marvelous love, for his miracle mercy to the children he loves. He poured great draughts of water down parched throats; the starved and hungry got plenty to eat.

(Ps. 107:8–9 MSG)

⚓ MY BOLD THOUGHTS

· ·

· ·

· ·

· ·

· ·

· ·

· ·

· ·

· ·

· ·

· ·

· ·

BOLD LOVE AND FORGIVENESS - Week 16
THE FINGERPRINTS OF LOVE

Cynthia

Smudgy little marks on my windows. I don't want to wipe them off because they remind me of a blue-eyed dolly with curly red hair whom I love with all my heart. As she pressed her chubby little face and fingers against the window, she squealed with delight and expressed with her own two-year-old vocabulary the beauty and wonder on the other side of the glass. How could I possibly wash that off?

As I looked through the smudged glass, I thought about the fingerprints we leave on the lives of others. We might not visibly see them, as on the glass of my windows, but they are indelibly marked with our words and actions. The good, the bad, our greatest and our worst moments leave marks on the people we do life with. Love, grace, forgiveness and our choices rub off day in and day out.

My grandmother left her indelible fingerprints on my life that have shaped much of who I am. I don't know if she thought about it much, but she lived and breathed out the faithfulness of God to those she touched. She was kind, gracious, and generous with all she possessed, soft-spoken, full of wisdom, and knew how to make you feel as if you were the most important person in the world. She was a Jesus lover and walked her faith out with quiet gentleness, never pushy or self-righteous, never shaming or belittling in her correction. She oozed love. Her fingerprints of grace and beauty on my life have forever marked my soul. I want to be just like her and leave the same kind of legacy for my grandchildren.

I know the choices I make every day become my influence. My influence will outlive my life. That is why it is so important to choose what kind of fingerprints I am going to leave and where I leave them.

I want to leave loving fingerprints everywhere. They might be invisible right now, but someday they will be visible on the lives I've been entrusted to love, nurture, and bless.

So I think I am going to clean my windows, but I'll just wipe around that little circle of smudged fingerprints, for now.

 BOLD ACTION STEP

Think about the kind of fingerprints you want to leave on the lives of others. Who are the recipients of your fingerprints? Write down the character qualities that express those fingerprints and pray for God to grow his fingerprint of love in your heart.

 VERSE OF THE WEEK

Be on your guard; stand firm in the faith; be courageous; be strong. Do everything in love.

(1 Cor. 16:13–14 NIV)

⚓ MY BOLD THOUGHTS

. . . .

. . . .

. . . .

. . . .

. . . .

. . . .

. . . .

. . . .

. . . .

. . . .

. . . .

. . . .

BOLD LOVE AND FORGIVENESS - Week 17
HEALING FOR THE HEART

Andrea

Did you know your heart is a muscle? A muscle must be stretched for it to get stronger. Any bodybuilder or fitness guru will tell you that. A muscle is broken down and then built back up; each time, it gets stronger and stronger.

Did you know our brain is a muscle too? The more we use it, the more intelligent we will become.

How about your heart? Does the same apply here? Let's think about our hearts for a minute. How many times has yours been broken? I know mine has felt like it's been stretched and ripped apart at times.

But then one morning, I woke up and it didn't hurt so bad anymore. My heart's been healed and it's becoming stronger every day.

For many years, I thought it was the responsibility of the people who hurt me to heal my heart, but I was wrong. The only one who can truly heal my heart is Jesus Christ. When I made a choice to stop being angry, the bitterness was replaced with compassion.

When I'm struggling, I ask God to help me see the other person through his eyes.

Apologizing doesn't always mean you're wrong and the other person is right; it means you value your relationship more than your ego.

Our hearts may feel pulled and stretched. Sometimes God's purpose in this is that we look inward.

Will you get real with God this week? He already knows; he's just waiting to hear it from you. It's easy to extend forgiveness to others, yet harder to give to ourselves. When we use our heart muscle to do its job of forgiving, we can walk *boldly* in freedom.

Adversity will always be something we will face. We can't always control what's happening around us, but we should challenge ourselves daily to control our response to what's happening. Our true character is seen in the face of adversity.

 BOLD ACTION STEP

Take a bold step this week and ask God to show you your heart. Is there something that needs to change in you? Is there someone you need to forgive; maybe yourself?

 VERSE OF THE WEEK

Now the Lord is the Spirit, and where the Spirit of the Lord is, there is freedom.

(2 Cor. 3:17 NIV)

MY BOLD THOUGHTS

. . . .

. . . .

. . . .

. . . .

. . . .

. . . .

. . . .

. . . .

. . . .

. . . .

. . . .

. . . .

CHAPTER FIVE

Bold Prayer

INTRODUCTION
PRAYING FOR THE WRONG REASONS

Cynthia

I WAS IN MY early twenties when I attended my first of many prayer seminars. We were challenged to pray an hour a day—and this was before I had children. I tried my best, but after a few weeks, I failed.

Over the next several years I heard more speakers talk about prayer and various methods we could use to infuse our prayer life.

I failed at all of them.

It took me a long time to realize my prayer should come out of my relationship with God. It isn't something I strive to perform so a box can be checked off.

I used to imagine God having a large chart with my name on it. When I failed to pray my hour a day, didn't use the seven-step method to effective prayer, or couldn't follow another methodology, he would put a big red *X* next to my name. He would sigh and shake his head in disappointment.

Of course, I know now this is a lie, but seeing God this way drove me to pray for all the wrong reasons. Instead of seeing prayer as a conversation with God because of my relationship with him, I saw it as finishing a chore so I could get God's approval. It took many years to overcome this lie and to learn to sit in my Father's lap and talk to him because I love him. I have come to understand that prayer is spending time with God, not because I want his approval, but because I need his love, mercy, wisdom, truth, and more, every minute and every second of the day.

BOLD PRAYER - Week 18
WRONG NUMBER

Andrea

As I was working on my laptop, I received a call from my daughter who said my two-month-old granddaughter had a mild fever and wouldn't eat much. My daughter sent pictures of my granddaughter's diaper. I will spare you the details; let's just say it didn't look normal.

My daughter got in to see a pediatrician, and after a brief examination, the doctor recommended my granddaughter be taken to the emergency room as soon as possible.

The emergency room doctor admitted her and began to run further tests.

Knowing the power in prayer, I reached out to my tribe of prayer warriors. I didn't know I would touch someone's life in the process.

I have a friend who is a nurse and lives over 2,000 miles away. I thought she could shed some light on the situation, so I sent her a text message along with the pictures my daughter sent me—even the diaper one.

I got a link back with information and a message saying she was praying for us.

About ten minutes later, I got a text back from her asking, "Who do you think this is?"

I paused for a moment and thought, *Please don't tell me this is someone else.*

She said, "I just got this phone number two months ago."

I had sent a total stranger diaper pictures!

I apologized for the mix-up and she said, "No problem." She then told me how much she loved kids, but sadly was unable to have any more children herself. She shared a heartbreaking testimony with me about her two babies in heaven. We continued texting for another few minutes about God and life, and I invited her to join our Live Bold Series Facebook group.

As we said goodnight, we promised to continue to pray for each other. My new friend sent me a text message the following day telling me she was praying that my granddaughter would have a restful day.

My grandbaby was diagnosed with salmonella poisoning and spent two days in the hospital. We don't know how it happened, but days earlier I had hosted our family's annual Christmas-cookie baking day, and someone may have handled raw eggs and forgot to wash their hands.

Was it a coincidence that I texted the wrong person? Not a chance. I don't doubt for a second this was all part of God's plan. This text message mix-up was a reminder that God listens as a concerned parent surely would. You see, when we bring our requests before God, he has three answers: "Yes," "Wait," or "I have something better." When she reached out to pray for us, God also put her on my heart. I prayed for help, and not only did God heal my granddaughter, but I was able to pray for someone else.

 BOLD ACTION STEP

Think of a time God answered your prayer in a way that was not necessarily the way you asked. Write about it and spend some time thanking him for his faithfulness. This week step outside your comfort zone. Be bold and speak truth to someone you don't already know. It can be a compliment, encouraging words, or sharing your faith. Write about your experience this week.

 VERSE OF THE WEEK

For where two or three gather in my name, there am I with them.

(Matt. 18:20 NIV)

⚓ MY BOLD THOUGHTS

· ·

· ·

· ·

· ·

· ·

· ·

· ·

· ·

· ·

· ·

· ·

· ·

BOLD PRAYER - Week 19
TRUTH AND LIES

Cynthia

When I was a little girl and got in trouble, I often heard, "Wait until your father comes home." Because I heard this continually, I would withdraw and hide from my dad.

By projecting the image I had of my own father, I learned to see God as someone who was mostly angry with me and waiting to get me. I realize even now at times, I hide from God when I am afraid or think he won't accept me or forgive me. I built a false image of God in my heart that keeps me from praying.

Once I released that image, I learned I could come to God as the writer of Hebrews tells us to—"So let us come boldly to the throne of our gracious God" (Heb. 4:16 NLT).

Albert Haase says in his book *Living the Lord's Prayer*, "Our image of God is one of the most, if not *the* most, important aspects of our spiritual formation. Our God-image shapes and colors everything about our personal spirituality, from why we pray to how we understand personal suffering and evil in the world."

Maybe you too have created a false image of God that keeps you from the rich intimacy of prayer with God. Look at this list and circle any false image of God you realize you've adopted:

Arbitrary dictator
Divine traffic cop
Chess master
Puppeteer
Divine trickster

Warden

Tyrant

Controller

Now that we've identified our false images of God, how can we be free of that image so we can enter into communion and prayer with God? The answer might surprise you. *Pray!* To correct the false image of God we have constructed in our minds, we need to pray the truth over the falsehoods. The Bible has treasures of promises of the true image of God. Once you start digging to find them and praying these verses, it will begin to shape a new image of God in you and change the way you pray.

 BOLD ACTION STEP

Find at least five scriptures about God's character and start praying them daily. Post them somewhere you can see them during the day—on the bathroom mirror, in the car, by the kitchen sink—anywhere you know you will bump into them each day.

 VERSE OF THE WEEK

So let us come boldly to the throne of our gracious God. There we will receive his mercy, and we will find grace to help us when we need it most.

(Heb. 4:16 NLT)

MY BOLD THOUGHTS

· ·

· ·

· ·

· ·

· ·

· ·

· ·

· ·

· ·

· ·

· ·

· ·

BOLD PRAYER - Week 20
STINKIN' THINKIN'

Andrea

I want to share a victory with you! But let me start with the struggle.

When I am hurt, upset, or angry, I isolate. It affects the people closest to me and often, the innocent bystanders. A good friend of mine calls it "Stinkin' Thinkin'."

After a long day at work and an intense Bible study at church, I had just gotten home. It was pushing 10:00 p.m., and I still wanted to finish my devotional from the morning.

I curled up on the couch with my favorite blanket, opened my Bible, and started to pray. My husband walked in the living room and saw me sitting on the couch and asked, "What are you doing?"

I responded with, "I need to read some truth, because I have a bad attitude!"

The look on his face was truly priceless. He said, "OK, Babe, I'll leave you alone. I love you!"

No hiding, no isolating, and no retreating! I did it. I admitted the truth instead of denying I had the issue. My husband showed me grace and let me have my space.

About an hour earlier during the Bible study we talked about the power of God. If he could make creation with the sound of his voice, surely he could change our situations. He has the power, so why doesn't he?

Maybe he's trying to grow our character or teach us important lessons, like Romans 5:3–5 (ESV) says.

Not only that, but we rejoice in our sufferings, knowing that suffering produces endurance, and endurance produces character, and character produces hope, and hope does not put us to shame, because God's love has been poured into our hearts through the Holy Spirit who has been given to us.

My bad attitude started as soon as I walked through my front door. I missed our sweet Doberman, Bella, we had put down a few weeks earlier. I had come home rewinding my to-do list over and over in my head and felt overwhelmed.

I know the things that make me vulnerable, like being overtired from not getting the proper amount of sleep, for starters. I should know better.

If you've walked the "bad attitude" road recently, do yourself a favor. Get on your knees and ask God for courage and strength to get through this season of your life. When the enemy is working overtime, miracles are right around the corner, because a thief doesn't steal from empty vaults. God is on the move and is up to something. Hang on!

 BOLD ACTION STEP

Think about the last time you had a bad attitude. How did you handle it? Did you brush it off and justify your actions, or did you pray and ask for help?

 VERSE OF THE WEEK

God met me more than halfway, he freed me from my anxious fears. Look at him; give him your warmest smile. Never hide your feelings from him. When I was desperate, I called out, and God got me out of a tight spot. God's angel sets up a circle of protection around us while we pray. Open your mouth and taste, open your eyes and see—how good God is. Blessed are you who run to him.

(Ps. 34:4–8 MSG)

⚓ MY BOLD THOUGHTS

BOLD PRAYER - Week 21
THE LEGACY OF PRAYER

Cynthia

My grandmother had a small table in her kitchen pushed up against the wall by the window. In the corner of her table sat her Bible, a devotional, and a notebook she kept her prayer requests written in. The visual picture is etched in my mind. More importantly, the memories of her prayers are written in my heart. Those prayers have become a part of the legacy she has left her grandchildren.

When we pray, it isn't just for us, but it is for those closest to us. They are the beneficiaries of our prayers. Because my grandmother prayed for me, it left an indelible mark for me to learn to pray for my family.

As a young mom, I realized the far-reaching effect prayer could have on my children. I began to pray for their futures. I prayed for the choices they would make for college, careers, and their wives. My grandmother's legacy of prayer gave me courage to pray bold prayers for my children and their future.

I am happy to report God has answered these many prayers amid both triumph and struggle. I have seen God shape my children's lives in ways I never had dreamed.

I don't consider myself a prayer warrior like my grandmother, but she taught me by example the importance of praying, because I *knew* she prayed. There were times in my life I sensed I was the recipient of her prayers, and it made a significant impact.

When my husband and I were struggling in the first few years of marriage, she was praying.

When I had trouble conceiving our second child, she was praying.

When I faced loss and depression, I witnessed the answer to her prayers. I received encouragement and strength from her prayers.

When I became a grandmother, I realized prayer would be the most meaningful gift I could give my grandchildren.

I prayed whispers of hopes and dreams for their lives.

Prayers of requests for their futures

Prayers of protection

Prayer for wisdom for their parents

Prayers that they would love Jesus with all their breath.

The legacy of prayer lives on through another generation. My hope and prayer is that I will be faithful to pray so my children and grandchildren will continue the legacy of prayer in our family.

 BOLD ACTION STEP

Make a list of bold prayers you want to see answered for those closest to you. Find a verse of scripture to pray with your request. Each day this week, pray one bold prayer and the scripture you have chosen for each person on your list.

 VERSE OF THE WEEK

Pray in the Spirit at all times and on every occasion. Stay alert and be persistent in your prayers for all believers everywhere.

(Eph. 6:18 NLT)

⚓ MY BOLD THOUGHTS

....

....

....

....

....

....

....

....

....

....

....

BOLD PRAYER - Week 22
WHEN THE STORY'S NOT OVER

Andrea

It was 4:00 a.m. and I had been writing since early in the morning. We were down to the last few days and the deadline was approaching for this devotional. I searched my computer for previous material I had written and came across a blog post I had written on August 31, 2012.

Some of you may know I entered two of my previous blogs in a writing contest tonight. As I sat in the parking lot waiting for my son's football practice to end, I thought I'd take advantage of the time to make some final changes before I sent it to another writer to edit. I walked in the door at 8:35 p.m., and after making the final touches, off they went at 8:57 p.m. with three whole minutes to spare. Sometimes I put the "Pro" in procrastination. I know there will be many amazing entries submitted, and I'm OK if mine are not chosen. If I had the opportunity to change one heart with my words, then that is a sweet VICTORY for me. It had been almost a year since I had written anything. During this writing break, I prayed God would guide my writing in the direction that brings him honor. I know there were things I needed to learn before I pursued more writing. He pressed upon my heart that he wants to be the first one I turn to in times of need. Not a friend, spouse, Google, Siri, or a self-help book. God wants our WHOLE hearts, not just the small part we're willing to share. When he created us, he carved out a place just for him. He is a jealous God because he created us for the sole purpose of worshiping him. Do you have a NO VACANCY sign hanging on the door to your heart?

I fought back the tears as I read what I had written five years earlier. Not long after this post, God took me on a journey of self-discovery, forgiveness, healing, and reconciliation. I understand why so much time passed before I became an author. My story was still being written.

Father God, thank you for never giving up on my hopes and dreams. Thank you for showing me you couldn't take me to the next level in my writing until I fixed my eyes completely on you. Help me keep them on you. Should I drift away, pull me back, Father, like a shepherd runs after his sheep. I pray my words bring you honor and my story brings you glory.

 BOLD ACTION STEP

Are you waiting for the fulfillment of your dreams? This week, get quiet with God as you wait and ask him to show you what he wants you to learn.

 VERSE OF THE WEEK

Therefore, my dear brothers and sisters, stand firm. Let nothing move you. Always give yourselves fully to the work of the Lord, because you know that your labor in the Lord is not in vain.

(1 Cor. 15:58 NIV)

⚓ MY BOLD THOUGHTS

. . . .

. . . .

. . . .

. . . .

. . . .

. . . .

. . . .

. . . .

. . . .

. . . .

. . . .

. . . .

CHAPTER SIX

Bold Compassion

INTRODUCTION
ANTIDOTE TO ANGER

Andrea

HAVE YOU SEEN THE movie *War Room*? If not, I highly recommend it. I saw it in the theater when it came out, but I recently came across it again while searching for something to watch on TV, and watched it again. Afterwards, I purchased a video and made myself a promise to watch it once a month for the entire year.

Why? I don't ever want to forget how powerful the gift of compassion can be. Compassion stops anger dead in its tracks. It's an antidote to anger.

Showing compassion can be difficult, but if we continue to carry bitterness and resentment from unresolved anger, our spiritual growth is crippled. Anger can keep us from our highest potential.

This week we hope you learn to see others the way Jesus does, through his eyes.

When we can look at others through the eyes of Jesus, something incredible happens. Our hearts become softer, our words become kinder, and our actions more loving.

As we start this chapter together, ask Jesus to prepare your heart so others may see his.

BOLD COMPASSION - Week 23
LEAKING COMPASSION

Cynthia

I walked out of the restaurant with my friend, as a woman with a child in her arms approached us. She was begging us for milk for her little boy. Begging wasn't uncommon in this area of Phnom Penh, Cambodia, where poverty is rampant and people from the surrounding villages come to the city for help out of desperation.

I saw the intense pain in the mother's face as my friend encouraged me to hand her my leftover sandwich. The woman bowed several times in humble gratitude.

Shocked, I had never seen anything like this. Not because a mother was begging for milk for her child, but because her child was grossly deformed from a condition called hydrocephalus, where the head swells to abnormal proportions.

Compassion leaked out of me like an overflowing river. I wanted to grab this mom and her child and take them to a doctor. I learned from my friend who is a missionary nurse that these conditions are common in countries like Cambodia.

My heart felt wrecked that day. I thought of my own three boys and how healthy they are because of the medical services we have back home. I wrestled with God that night as I processed all I had seen on the dirty streets in the villages and the city. It didn't seem fair. I cried out to God, "Why? Why was I born in a place where my children have potential to thrive physically and flourish emotionally?"

I was moved to take responsibility for the many privileges I have. I had a gift of resources, and I needed to apply them with compassion to help others.

The compassion I wrestled with propelled me to take action when I got back home. I shared with Kevin what I saw, and we immediately decided to sponsor two children from Cambodia.

It is overwhelming when we see needs we can't meet. Everyone can do something when moved by compassion. I know I can't help everyone, but I can make a difference in two little lives in that part of the world.

Jesus was moved with great compassion as he traveled in and out of villages. Jesus spoke and touched the lepers whom others regarded as unclean. To be unclean meant that you were ostracized and sent to live outside of the village with no contact from the outside world. Leprosy didn't stop Jesus from showing love and mercy. Blindness, deformities, diseases, and mental illness didn't keep Jesus from extending compassion. He knew compassion brings hope and healing.

My compassion badge isn't always in evidence. I pray I will always remember when my heart was wrecked in Cambodia and extend compassion when God whispers to me to take a bold step in response to great need.

➤ BOLD ACTION STEP

You may not have visited a country like Cambodia, but can you think of a place in your part of the world where you can show compassion? I have a friend who keeps granola bars in her car to hand out when she sees people begging at an intersection or parking lot. Be aware this week of your surroundings and how you can exercise bold compassion to bring hope and healing to someone who needs it. Take a bold step to act with compassion.

 VERSE OF THE WEEK

Praise be to the God and Father of our Lord Jesus Christ, the Father of compassion and the God of all comfort, who comforts us in all our troubles, so that we can comfort those in any trouble with the comfort we ourselves receive from God.

(2 Cor. 1:3–4 NIV)

⚓ MY BOLD THOUGHTS

. . . .

. . . .

. . . .

. . . .

. . . .

. . . .

. . . .

. . . .

. . . .

. . . .

. . . .

BOLD COMPASSION - Week 24
ASSUMPTIONS AND INTENTIONS

Andrea

A woman was driving to work and noticed in her rearview mirror a car coming up behind her very quickly. The car was weaving in and out of traffic and driving erratically. As the driver maneuvered his way around her, he barely missed the back of her car as he sped by. She hit her brakes and spilled her coffee on her new blouse. Frustrated and angry, she couldn't understand how someone could be so careless.

The next morning, the same thing happened. A driver was weaving in and out of traffic and driving erratically. Again, as he maneuvered his way around her and as he sped by, he almost hit the back of her car. Just then, the traffic light ahead turned red. Just as she was about to roll down her window to speak her mind, she noticed a woman sobbing in the back seat, holding what appeared to be a young girl. The woman had a towel around the girl's leg, and she could see it was covered with blood.

In the first scenario, the careless driver may have overslept and doesn't want to be late for work. The second scenario was a father rushing his three-year-old daughter to the hospital two blocks away because she severed her leg on a lawnmower blade. Although the father's motive was different in the second scenario, his actions were the same.

I make this point because we all do this. We see similar behavior from people and assume their motives are the same. When we think we know another person's intentions, we may be basing it on a hunch or an assumption based on past behavior.

Since God is the only one who can see inside the heart, we don't really know. We can't judge people by their actions and then judge ourselves by our intentions. Thankfully, God sees our hearts and he judges accordingly. He knows how deeply we desire to please him.

Just last night, I had a bad attitude as I was feeling overwhelmed about getting things done before leaving for a writer's conference with Cynthia in the morning. I shared with my husband what I was feeling, which included my twisted need for everything to be perfect. This is both a blessing and a curse, people! I wanted to clean up the house before I left, change the sheets, and have dinner made before my husband got home, and I still had to pack for a five-day trip to North Carolina, with just a carry-on suitcase! Normally a carry-on is for my shoes, not a five-day wardrobe! The twelve-degree weather forecast for the area called for bulky winter clothes, close to impossible to cram into a tiny suitcase.

My husband reassured me and said, "Give yourself some grace." I was letting perfectionism and fear of failure rule me. I was discouraged because I wanted to have dinner ready so we could have a nice dinner before I left. But it didn't play out the way I saw it in my head.

The good thing is, it's not in the act of doing itself. When our actions stem from the right motives, God is still pleased.

BOLD ACTION STEP

This week ask God to bring someone to mind that you need to show more compassion toward and less irritation toward. Ask the Lord, "Help me see _____ (add name) through your eyes and not my own."

VERSE OF THE WEEK

Therefore let us not pass judgment on one another any longer, but rather decide never to put a stumbling block or hindrance in the way of a brother.

(Rom. 14:13 ESV)

MY BOLD THOUGHTS

· ·

· ·

· ·

· ·

· ·

· ·

· ·

· ·

· ·

· ·

· ·

BOLD COMPASSION - Week 25
INCONVENIENT COMPASSION

Cynthia

An unprecedented snowstorm in Atlanta caused a delay in my flight home for nearly thirty hours. Andrea and I were coming back from a marketing conference in North Carolina in the middle of January. Ironically, Andrea's flight left on time because her connection involved a city that wasn't impacted.

My flights were cancelled so many times I lost track. I had a stack of boarding passes that rotated like a Ferris wheel as I tried to follow which flights were delayed or cancelled. I felt like I was living the movie *Groundhog Day* where the same events keep repeating themselves. I just wanted to go home, but felt I was stuck in a time warp of events and couldn't catch a break.

When travel plans change, the stress level heightens. I have great respect for the airline personnel, from those on the ground to those who serve in the air. I empathize with the customer service agents because they had to apologize for events they couldn't control.

Weather can't be controlled, but our perspective can. As I listened to some cranky people around me, I made a choice to adjust my attitude. I was determined to offer compassion to those serving us. In case you get the wrong impression, I didn't get to that place right away. I had to verbally talk myself through. "What is the worst that can happen? It's not the end of the world," I told myself as I adjusted my schedule and waited. After I prayed and asked God to help me, I could see beyond myself and offer compassion to those who were trying to help me get home.

When boarding the last flight, I learned the crew had already been working way over their allotted hours, and they too were weary and just wanted to go home. A bond of understanding was forged between the crew and the passengers because we all wanted the same thing—to go home!

I learned that compassion goes beyond empathy in a situation like this. Compassion in its highest form has to involve action. It isn't always convenient. It doesn't always feel good. It isn't always comfortable, and it often means sacrifice and giving up something.

Jesus had compassion. It wasn't at an airport terminal, but it was among a mass of people. "When he saw the crowds, he had compassion for them, because they were harassed and helpless, like sheep without a shepherd" (Matt. 9:36 ESV).

His compassion went beyond just feeling bad for them. His compassion was activated by mercy and motivated to action. When we understand the gift of mercy we have been given by God, we can extend compassion with action to others.

 BOLD ACTION STEP

Next time you find yourself in a situation where your plans are interrupted, think about how you can move from just *feeling* compassion to *acting* with compassion. This week ask God to heighten your awareness toward acting boldly with compassion.

 VERSE OF THE WEEK

As a father shows compassion to his children, so the Lord shows compassion to those who fear him.

(Ps. 103:13 ESV)

⚓ MY BOLD THOUGHTS

. . . .

. . . .

. . . .

. . . .

. . . .

. . . .

. . . .

. . . .

. . . .

. . . .

. . . .

. . . .

BOLD COMPASSION - Week 26
PAYING ATTENTION

Andrea

My husband came home as I was unloading the car with colorful flowers to plant. In a playful voice he said, "Oh, I see—more victims!"

Sad, but it was true. I have never had a green thumb. I've always wished I did.

For my birthday, my husband bought me an indoor Aero Garden with Thai basil, oregano, cilantro, and dill. I was so excited not to have to buy any more herbs to cook with. This was my chance to prove I could keep a plant alive. My husband set it up, programmed the lights, and added the minerals. The alarm would even signal when more water needed to be added.

Within a few weeks, I had more herbs than I knew what to do with. I was so proud of myself! I frequently shared the herbs with friends who stopped by and bring them to work.

Recently, I looked at my little garden and noticed it looked a bit sparse. Leaves were barely hanging on, and some had dried up and completely fallen off. My heart sank as I thought, *With the easiest garden on the planet, you still can't keep a plant alive.* I opened the water reservoir and discovered there was no water. Not a single drop. Strangely, I felt relieved there was a logical explanation.

Just like a garden, our relationships suffer when we don't pay attention to them. When we withhold attention (whether intentional or not), relationships die emotionally. We pay more attention to our cell phones and checking how many social media likes we have, than growing relationships with our spouses, children, and grandchildren. If you are reading this and feeling convicted, you're not alone, and neither am I!

The second part is not so easy to fix. It's called the "dome zone" or the after effect. When the pods are first placed in the Aero Garden, they need to be covered with a plastic dome for the first few weeks until the herbs start to bud. Once they get to be an inch or so tall, the domes can be removed to allow the light to help them grow.

I thought about what happens to us once our "dead leaves" start to fall off. We want to rise above and try again, but a wall surrounds our hearts. Like the dome shield, we think it is protecting us so no one can hurt us again. We fail to realize that although growth can be seen in the beginning, if we don't remove the dome the herbs will eventually intertwine. As a result, since there is no room to grow, the plants strangle themselves.

Somewhere I read, "Comfort zones are nice places to visit, but nothing ever grows there." Don't give up. Fight for the relationships important to you. After thirty years of marriage, we're still growing as a couple and I'm still learning to be the wife God has called me to be.

 BOLD ACTION STEP

What relationships come to mind this week that need tending? What bold step will you take this week to show the people in your life they are important?

 VERSE OF THE WEEK

And let us not grow weary of doing good, for in due season we will reap, if we do not give up.

(Gal. 6:9 ESV)

⚓ MY BOLD THOUGHTS

CHAPTER SEVEN

Bold Service

INTRODUCTION
SERVING TOGETHER

Cynthia

RUMMAGING THROUGH SOME OLD bins in the garage, we found a vintage scrapbook belonging to my husband's father when he was in the service. Pages and pages reveal the many assignments he took as a pilot in WW II and the Korean War. Kevin never knew his dad; he died tragically in a plane crash on one of his last missions before he was to take a post as a schoolteacher. We also found notes and cards sharing acts of service to his wife and family. The legacy his father left was one of service, the sacrificial kind.

I often think of my father-in-law and others in his generation as men and women who served boldly. Their service was purposeful and it bonded them together both in pre- and post-war times. There was a sense of rallying together in serving sacrificially, but also harnessing their gifts for a common goal.

Serving is something everyone can do. It isn't limited to a few. It isn't limited to one generation such as that of our parents or grandparents. We all can serve.

In this chapter, we'll look at how God has called us each to serve intentionally so we can leave a bold legacy of service to others.

BOLD SERVICE - Week 27
DUCT TAPE AND CRACKED PLACES

Cynthia

The other night when I opened the fridge, my favorite summer tray fell off the top and I had to catch it before it hit me squarely in the face. Underneath the place mat on the tray I noticed some extra decorating. Duct tape! Did Kevin think I wouldn't notice? The tray had obviously been involved in some sort of an accident. My sweet man had tried to repair the crack.

"What happened to my favorite tray? Were you trying to hide it?" I asked, nicely, of course.

"No, I wasn't trying to keep it from you. It just happened! But I fixed it for you." *Sigh.* how could I be irritated with that answer? He was trying to fix it for me!

I have struggled wanting to keep my faults and broken places covered up under the placemat of my life, trying to give my tray a more perfect appearance. When I try to cover up my brokenness and wounds by camouflaging them, hoping no one will notice, it doesn't work out very well. When I do this it makes me feel disqualified to serve others. The fact is, we are all broken. We have scars, we have wounds, and we have trauma, anxiety, hurts, and difficult challenges.

If we want to serve boldly, you and I will have to lift off the "place mats" attempting to cover the cracked places of our lives and expose the brokenness and wounds.

My favorite tray can't serve anyone unless it is carried. It doesn't serve by itself. Thank you, Jesus; it is you who carries my imperfect life and offers the heart of your message to serve others.

➤ BOLD ACTION STEP

Where do you need to have God carry you today so you too can serve? Make your duct-tape list of imperfections. Go ahead—ask God to remove that place mat from the tray of your life and mend the broken place so you can bless and serve others today and every day.

♡ VERSE OF THE WEEK

My grace is enough to cover and sustain you. My power is made perfect in weakness. *So ask me about my thorn*, inquire about my weaknesses, and I will gladly go on and on—*I would rather stake my claim in these* and have the power of the Anointed One at home within me. I am at peace *and even take pleasure* in any weaknesses, insults, hardships, persecutions, and afflictions for the sake of the Anointed because when I am at my weakest, He makes me strong.

(2 Cor. 12:9–10 TV)

MY BOLD THOUGHTS

BOLD SERVICE - Week 28
THE JOURNEY OF SERVICE

Andrea

My husband and I own a towing and transportation company in Northern California. In 2008, my husband had an idea to bring the community together while at the same time blessing the less fortunate children in our community during Christmas. He planned to invite the local towing companies to come together and caravan together about fourteen miles to our church. It is a sight to see them going down the freeway with their lights and flashers on.

Each year since, the tow trucks big and small pull into our church for a parade featuring Santa Claus in a sleigh on the back of a flatbed. We provide a buffet breakfast, a toy drive, and a raffle. Last year, we donated over eight hundred toys to children in our community.

It all started with an idea. We never thought it would grow to be the size it is today. Helped by like-minded people, God's Tow Truck Toy Run has turned into something bigger than we could ever have imagined.

Did you know we are all called to service? Galatians 5:13 (NIV) says, "You, my brothers and sisters, were called to be free. But do not use your freedom to indulge the flesh; rather, serve one another humbly in love."

How can you find an area where you can be of service?

- Think about the things you are good at, then reach out to friends who share the same desire to serve.
- What are you passionate about?

Your answer to these questions can start you on your journey of service. God places hopes, dreams, and desires in our hearts, knowing he will use them to bring himself glory. In 1 Corinthians 10:3b (NIV) it says, "Whatever you do, do it for the glory of God."

Team up with people who share your same hopes and dreams. Surround yourself with people who are passionate about the same things you are. Everyone has something to contribute to this world.

We need community. We need each other. but serving is much more fun when we're doing it with like-minded people together.

 BOLD ACTION STEP

What are your strengths? What are you good at? Grab a friend this week who shares the same passions, and brainstorm ways you can give back to your community. Then go out and make a difference. Keep track of your dreams, plans, and projects and keep working on them.

 VERSE OF THE WEEK

God is not unjust; he will not forget your work and the love you have shown him as you have helped his people and continue to help them.

(Heb. 6:10 NIV)

MY BOLD THOUGHTS

BOLD SERVICE - Week 29
LIFE IN THE DASH

Cynthia

On occasion, I enjoy walking through a cemetery and reading the epitaphs. While I learn names and dates, I often wonder what happened in a person's life between the two numbers—what happened in between the dash.

The dash between when we were born and when we die represents the amazing race God has called us to run.

The race is ours to run and ours alone. It's not the amount of time we are given, but what we do with the gift of time we are given. Our dash represents our service and how we lived out our purpose. That's all we are responsible for, nothing more, nothing less.

How will you live your dash, whatever part of it is left?

Hebrews 12:1 gives us a clue of how we can be sure to run the race and serve boldly. It says first we have an example, "a great cloud of witnesses"—those who have gone before us. As we look to their faithfulness, we gain courage to keep on serving and running our race.

Next it says we are to "lay aside every weight," or in other words, strip off the extra weight. The Message Bible says the same verse well:

> Do you see what this means—all these pioneers who blazed the way, all these veterans cheering us on? It means we'd better get on with it. Strip down, start running—and never quit! No extra spiritual fat, no parasitic sins.

A parasite is something that lives off its host in the body. It sometimes is very difficult to get rid of. We might even refer to it as a stronghold.

A sin in our lives that has a stronghold is like a parasite as it feeds off the cycles of our behavior. Sounds disgusting, doesn't it? The simile here is strong because God desires for you and me to run our race well without any obstacles.

The crown of these verses follows: "Looking to Jesus, the founder and perfecter of our faith" (Heb. 12:2 ESV). We don't have to do it all by ourselves! Jesus can help us live out our dash and serve successfully.

 BOLD ACTION STEP

What weights are holding you back from running your race? Ask God to show you what strongholds might be keeping you from serving successfully. If you are really bold, you can ask a close friend to help you identify something they might see holding you back. You can do it! Be bold and ask so you can grow.

 VERSE OF THE WEEK

Therefore, since we are surrounded by so great a cloud of witnesses, let us also lay aside every weight, and sin which clings so closely, and let us run with endurance the race that is set before us, looking to Jesus, the founder and perfecter of our faith.

(Heb. 12:1–2 ESV)

MY BOLD THOUGHTS

BOLD SERVICE - Week 30
OBEY THAT NUDGE

Andrea

I woke up craving my favorite omelet from a cute little restaurant on a quaint street near my home. I felt a strong urge to go have breakfast there, which I do frequently to write, catch up on emails, etc. Then I was reminded of a $100 bill I had been saving in my wallet for a rainy day.

You need to go today. Give whoever is waiting on you this money, I heard in my heart. When I hear God's voice, I know it's not up for negotiation. I believe we need to be obedient when we feel that nudge from bless someone.

I drove to the restaurant, walked in, and was seated at my favorite table. The owner saw me step in and began making my usual Iced Caramel Macchiato with whipped cream and chocolate sprinkles (a signature drink there).

After I caught up on a few personal tasks on my phone and had finished my yummy "Rafael" omelet with its linguiça, jalapeños, pepper-jack cheese, and spinach, it was time to be a blessing.

I motioned my waitress to my table. I told her, "I don't know your situation, but God does. He put you on my heart this morning." As I talked to her, I placed the nicely folded $100 bill in her hand.

She said, "Thank you, thank you," and went on to tell me that sometimes her customers didn't treat her very nicely. "When I got up this morning, I prayed God would help me have a good day."

Jesus can't be here in the flesh, but he sends his Holy Spirit to live inside us when we invite him in. Jesus told us that the most important thing we can do is to love him with all our hearts and to love others aboveas ourselves.

The Bible says, in Luke 12:48b (NIV), "From everyone who has been given much, much will be demanded; and from the one who has been entrusted with much, much more will be asked." Our money is not ours. It belongs to God. What's left after all your bills are paid? Could you use some of it to bring God glory? If you're willing, he will show you just how you can.

 BOLD ACTION STEP

What you've just read was my story. Ask God to show you yours. There are many ways you can be a blessing that doesn't involve money. Time is one of the most precious gifts you can give. How can you be a blessing to someone this week?

 VERSE OF THE WEEK

Do nothing from selfish ambition or conceit, but in humility count others more significant than yourselves. Let each of you look not only to his own interests, but also to the interests of others.

(Phil. 2: 3–4 ESV)

⚓ MY BOLD THOUGHTS

. . . .

. . . .

. . . .

. . . .

. . . .

. . . .

. . . .

. . . .

. . . .

. . . .

. . . .

BOLD SERVICE - Week 31
USING YOUR GIFTS

Cynthia

I blocked off my calendar all day today to do what I love. Write. But I have to admit it terrifies me! I know from the core of my being I am called to serve by putting words on a page, yet my mind plays tricks and tells me twisted lies. The little minions continue their rant of *You can't do it* or *It won't be good enough*, or *Who wants to read what you write?*

When we serve in our calling it can be agonizing and feel as if we are hiking up a mountain in 120-degree weather with a 100-pound pack on our backs. There are moments where the climb is easier, but it is still a push to move forward with sweat and yes, even tears! The exhilarating part of the climb is reaching the top of the summit. When we are finished, it is like standing on the highest mountain peak looking out at the magnificent panoramic view with gratefulness at being able to reach the top.

If we are honest, whether we are writers, speakers, leaders, teachers, coaches, or Sunday school teachers, expressing our gifts in service can be terrifying.

Here are a few things to remember as we serve:

- The gift isn't about *me*. It's about God. He is the giver of the gifts. I don't write to bless me; I write to bless others! My hope is my gift will draw people closer to the heart of Jesus and encourage them to live intentionally.

- I don't have to do it alone. God expects us to walk and live in community. Being a strong, independent person, I find it easy to fall into the trap of not asking for help. It's way more fun to have companions on the journey. When you get to the top, you have people to celebrate with you. Who wants to party all alone?

- God wants us to succeed; after all, he gave us the gifts in the first place to serve in his kingdom! You and I are responsible to unwrap the gift, take it out of the box and serve! Our gifts aren't meant to sit on a shelf or to hide in a closet. He gave you and me gifts for a purpose and he is our biggest cheerleader!

Let's stop whining, put on our packs and start climbing, putting one foot in front of the other, even if we are terrified. God promises to help us every step of the way as we seek to honor him with the gifts and the call he has given us.

 BOLD ACTION STEP

Have you, like me, been a little afraid to start using your gift? Be encouraged today to take that gift you have been hiding off the shelf and put it to use.

 VERSE OF THE WEEK

His divine power has given us everything we need for a godly life through our knowledge of him who called us by his own glory and goodness.

(2 Peter 1:3 NIV)

MY BOLD THOUGHTS

CHAPTER EIGHT

Bold Friendship

INTRODUCTION
A GATHERING OF THE TRIBE

Andrea

SHORTLY AFTER WE MOVED into our new home, I had my first "Tribe Party." They came from many facets of my life: from grade school to my professional career. There was no hiding my joy, as I introduced many of them for the first time. As a gift for my girls, I had bracelets made, each with three small hearts, representing the two of us, with God at the center.

I asked each tribe member to bring one thing that reminded them of our friendship. There was laughter and tears depending on the story they chose to share. Before the party was over, friend requests were sent through social media and many phone numbers were exchanged. It was a precious time I will always cherish.

It's not often someone tells you how you have impacted their life. And sometimes, without you even knowing.

How often do you tell your tribe members how they have influenced your life? It is our prayer that as you read these stories of friendship, that the Lord would bring a special friend to mind this week.

BOLD FRIENDSHIP - Week 32
GO-TO GIRLS

Andrea

My tribe. That's what I call my "go-to" girls. The one who planned a weekend getaway, then once she found out my birthday plans changed, canceled her trip, so I wouldn't spend my birthday alone. She's my partner in crime, my travel buddy, my person.

My tribe. She's the one who picks me up from the airport at all hours of the night, holds up a welcome sign to greet me, instead of waiting curbside to pick me up, she waits another ninety minutes for my luggage to hit the carousel.

My tribe. The one God brought into my life unexpectedly, at the perfect time. She tells me I'm her angel, but she's the real angel.

My tribe. The only one I've trusted for twenty-seven years to touch my hair, the one who would slay dragons for me.

My tribe. I've known her since I had a crush on Rusty in second grade. The one who loves me enough to tell me what I need to hear, not what I want to hear.

My tribe. The one who brought me into this world. I love you, Mom.

My tribe. She can help me turn an old piece of wood into a masterpiece.

My tribe. The one who always tells me she loves me extremely.

My tribe. She drove over an hour just to sit with me and pray.

My tribe. Before I ever spoke a word, she knew what I was feeling long before I ever did.

My tribe. She walked with me during the hardest journey of my life, then stood in the gap and believed for me until I was able.

My tribe. She's listened to my phone call rants at all hours of the night (added up, I'm sure they would be thousands of hours). She's the one who holds me accountable and knows me the best.

My tribe. The one who included me in her tribe and encouraged me to start a tribe of my own. Cynthia is the person I've looked up to and admired since I was a little girl. She is an encourager, a mentor, and the most God-fearing woman I've ever met. Her heart exemplifies a heart after Christ and it shows in her willingness to be obedient. She is a firstborn, a perfectionist and has a type-A personality—all like me. She taught me the importance of friendship at a young age and for that I will be forever grateful.

 BOLD ACTION STEP

Write a letter to two friends this week and share with them how they have influenced your life. Then, Sseriously consider throwing your own tribe party this year.

 VERSE OF THE WEEK

As iron sharpens iron, so a friend sharpens a friend.

(Prov. 27:17 NLT)

MY BOLD THOUGHTS

· ·

· ·

· ·

· ·

· ·

· ·

· ·

· ·

· ·

· ·

· ·

BOLD FRIENDSHIP - Week 33
FOCUS ON WHAT MATTERS

Cynthia

It was way past my bedtime. The phrase "leadership matters" was haunting me. Bill Hybels at the Global Leadership Summit said it repeatedly, "Leadership matters."

It was real to me in the moment because I got word that a very dear woman I knew in my distant past had just graduated to heaven. A mutual friend let me know she was moments away from eternity two days earlier and shared that I could text her to send an encouraging note. What should I say? It felt so fake, so insincere to come in at the eleventh hour when someone is dying.

I remembered how she had reached out to me a few times on social media to encourage me by saying how I had impacted her life ever so long ago. She didn't care that we hadn't talked for eons, it didn't bother her that we weren't at the same church anymore or even close friends, and she just wanted me to know. It was an act of true friendship because she had eternity in view.

It haunts me to think of the times I have carelessly thrown out words without regard to how they might impact others. And yet, this sweet soul was in the background watching my life and told me how blessed she was and I didn't even realize how much my leadership mattered.

There's one more thing that haunts me, words from Ephesians 4:1–2 (NLT) that I've been trying to commit to memory, "Lead a life worthy of your calling, for you have been called by God. Always be humble and gentle. Be patient with each other, making allowance for each other's faults because of your love."

These words from Paul, and the words of my distant friend who finished her race, propel me to intentionally focus on things in life that truly matter. I don't want to forget to embed deeper qualities in my soul like humility, gentleness, patience, and most of all to love people well. Because when all is said and done, loving matters. God says over and over again in his Book that it matters. I know I don't get it right all the time but I try to remember. Loving well matters. Our words matter. Friendship matters.

 BOLD ACTION STEP

Think of someone in your life who has influenced you and you haven't connected with lately. Take the time to him or her a note of thanks for the way they have impacted your life.

♡ **VERSE OF THE WEEK**

Therefore I, a prisoner for serving the Lord, beg you to lead a life worthy of your calling, for you have been called by God. Always be humble and gentle. Be patient with each other, making allowance for each other's faults because of your love.

(Eph. 4:1–2 NLT)

MY BOLD THOUGHTS

BOLD FRIENDSHIP - Week 34
GOD-BREATHED FRIENDSHIP

Andrea

When life knocked me to my knees, my friends who were going through their own struggles stood in the gap for me and encouraged me to believe God's Word, instead of what I was seeing with my own eyes. Because we are connected in Christ, I love them as my "own soul."

One of the best examples of a God-breathed friendship is the connection between David and Jonathan (1 Sam. 18–20). Jonathan was the son of Saul, the first king of Israel, and next in line for the throne. When King Saul disobeyed God and lost his kingdom, God chose David to be the next king of Israel instead.

Jonathan knew he would never be king, but still he befriended David. Jonathan wanted to obey God with all his heart, so he trusted God's decision to make David the next king. Can you imagine hanging out with the very person who took your kingdom, your inheritance, your throne? If Jonathan had not known God the way he did, he may have sided with his father and may have killed David himself.

Saul hated David because the Lord was with him. Despite his father's hatred of David, Jonathan and David became great friends. Best friends. When King Saul tried to kill David, Jonathan helped him escape.

My favorite part of the story says, "The soul of Jonathan was knit to the soul of David, and Jonathan loved him as his own soul" (1 Sam. 18:1 NKJV). Jonathan displayed true character and integrity toward his friend David.

BOLD ACTION STEP

Have you had to give up something to keep a friendship? Journal what feelings you experienced. Think about how you can honor a friend this week, like Jonathan did for David. Find a meaningful way to let your friend know you care.

 VERSE OF THE WEEK

There are "friends" who destroy each other, but a real friend sticks closer than a brother.

(Prov. 18:24 NLT)

⚓ MY BOLD THOUGHTS

....

....

....

....

....

....

....

....

....

....

....

....

BOLD FRIENDSHIP - Week 35
FIND WHERE YOU BELONG

Cynthia

As a writer, I floundered for a few years. I didn't know it but I was looking for my tribe. I had friends but I didn't have a tribe.

I searched and scoured to find a group I could identify with . . . a group whose heart beat the same as mine . . . writing words hoping to make a difference. I prayed and waited.

I tried to force myself with a few and it didn't work. It was like putting a square peg into a round hole. They were lovely, but weren't my peeps, so I kept looking and asking my writer friends. Mostly, I prayed and asked God to help me find my tribe; one I could feel camaraderie and affinity with.

And then I found my tribe. They were Jesus-loving writers, confident in their gifts and yet at times insecure, broken but not defeated, struggling and yet persevering, desiring and yet God honoring. It was like being away from home a long time and finding all the best reasons why you love to come back. It was a belonging moment.

Whatever gifts we might have, we need people who can be our tribe. Why? Here are five simple reasons:

- Trust—We need a group of people who we can trust with our gift and who can give us healthy feedback.
- Respect—People who share the same gift can motivate us to be the best we can be.
- Inspire—Being around other like-minded, similarly-gifted people is incredibly inspiring. It pushes us to work harder and smarter.

- Belong—When you discover your true tribe you will feel at home. With people who understand how your gift works you will have a safe place to grow and try out new ideas.
- Encourage—Everyone needs encouragement especially when our gifts are being developed and later when we've experienced both success and failure. We need people to remind us to keep stewarding the gift.

Jesus had disciples, they were friends and yet they were his tribe. Jesus handpicked each disciple who would grow together and share the same passion. Together they turned the world upside down, bringing a message of reconciliation and hope for eternity.

Who is your tribe?

➤ BOLD ACTION STEP

What is your gift? What is your calling? Do you have a tribe? Take a first step this week to identify your tribe. Somewhere out there is a place for you to belong and to grow that brilliant gift he has entrusted to you.

VERSE OF THE WEEK

For this reason I remind you to fan into flame the gift of God, which is in you through the laying on of my hands.

(2 Tim. 1:6 ESV)

⚓ MY BOLD THOUGHTS

. . . .

. . . .

. . . .

. . . .

. . . .

. . . .

. . . .

. . . .

. . . .

. . . .

. . . .

. . . .

CHAPTER NINE

Bold Trust

INTRODUCTION
SURRENDER AND TRUST

Andrea

TRUST IS THE FOUNDATION of every relationship. It can take a few minutes to destroy and years to rebuild. Yet there is hope. Jesus is our hope and he is trustworthy.

Like me, you may have had pieces of your heart scattered over lots of places. As a result, you may struggle to trust God.

There came a time when I knew I had to make a choice. I could no longer continue making the same choices while hoping for a different outcome. This, my friends, is the definition of insanity. I needed to fully surrender and trust God with my marriage, finances, my career, and most importantly, my heart!

Sometimes the things we want the most in life, aren't God's best for us. "And we know that in all things God works for the good of those who love him, who have been called according to his purpose" (Rom. 8:28 NIV). I knew it was time to let go of my will and give God permission to have complete control.

You can make the same choice I did to "let go and let God!" Will you choose to believe this week that God will make all things right, according to his will?

Both the dark and the light serve a purpose to shape us into who we are called to be. The lessons can be for you, someone you know, or maybe for someone who's watching. God wouldn't have allowed it if there wasn't good to be birthed from it. Why? Because God is *always* good and He is worthy of our trust.

BOLD TRUST - Week 36
BREATHE AND TRUST

Cynthia

Breathing is an automatic response that we rarely think about. Each breath is a reminder that we are alive. Each breath is a sign that life moves forward whether we will it or not.

When we experience pain so immediate and encompassing, it feels as though we can barely take a breath.

I've had moments when I've taken some deep breaths along the journey and exhaled, but at times the ruts and rough places on the path have caught my breath so much that I forget how to breathe.

You know that feeling when something catches you by surprise and you take a sharp breath in and then let out a panicky scream? It's a reaction to uncertainty or fear. It's like coming to a screeching stop because we've almost hit someone in a parking lot or when a scary part jumps across the movie screen. It takes time to begin to breathe normally again.

In the hard times, I can find myself forgetting to breathe as if I'm climbing up craggy hillsides or facing fierce storms. I am reluctant to say this, but I must confess, it sets me back and erodes my ability to trust in the one who gives me breath.

God. My Jesus, the one I've loved since I was a small child. Life seems to pile up in heaps and I am out of practice exhaling and consistently letting go. I think another word for letting go is surrender. You can't trust God if you don't surrender. God reminds me often and whispers, Let it go, so you can grow. The "it" are things I am trying to fix and failing miserably because I forget something very important. I am not God, it's not my job to fix, only to be faithful and follow. I need to trust.

C.S. Lewis said, pain is God's megaphone to the world. Through our pain, God longs to speak to you and to me. It is in the exhalation that the hurt and wounds get released. In other words, when we hold our breath, we can black out spiritually and emotionally. We need to breathe and trust. Breathe and trust.

 BOLD ACTION STEP

What do you need to let go of so you can trust God? What have you been trying to fix? Take the time to write a response to God in answer to these questions. Be gut honest. Tell God why you have trouble letting go and trusting. You can start right now, new and afresh, and begin trusting him so you can breathe!

 VERSE OF THE WEEK

You can be saved by returning to me. You can have rest. You can be strong by being quiet and by trusting me.

(Isa. 30:15 GW)

MY BOLD THOUGHTS

BOLD TRUST - Week 37
BROKEN TRUST

Andrea

When trust is broken, it can have a negative effect on all of our relationships. When I experienced betrayal, suddenly everyone seemed to be my worst enemy and no one was trustworthy. From misplacing my phone, to losing something in my house, I instantly thought someone had taken them.

Sadly, the relationship damaged the most was my relationship with Christ. I doubted him, and as a result, I worried and doubted just about everything. I felt the closeness I once had with Christ was severed. I didn't like who I was becoming. It was the complete opposite of who God made me to be. I went from giving everyone the benefit of the doubt and leading with my heart, to charging everyone as guilty before ever hearing their case.

Then I worried and doubted just about everything. I realized I couldn't fully trust God and worry at the same time.

Did you know God has the *already* to your *what if*? It's already taken care of! That problem at work coming up? Done. He has gone before you to fight battles you don't even know are coming. "If anyone pays attention to what they're taught, they will succeed. Blessed is the person who trusts in the Lord" (Prov. 16:20b NIRV).

Trusting God means letting go of our worries, anxieties, and the uncertainties of our future. It calls for complete surrender and trusting that God has our back. When we trust God, he shows us how all-powerful he is.

He can do whatever he wants, whenever he wants, however he wants, and to whomever he wants. But since he is a perfect gentleman, he will never force himself on us. We can trust him because he is always working things out for our good.

 **BOLD ACTION STEP**

Make a choice to believe God is working all things out for your good, no matter what comes your way this week. Write "God is Working it Out!" on a note and put it somewhere where you will see it throughout the day. Next, journal about a time when God turned something around for your good.

 **VERSE OF THE WEEK**

And again, "I will put my trust in him."

(Heb. 2:13 ESV)

⚓ MY BOLD THOUGHTS

. . . .

. . . .

. . . .

. . . .

. . . .

. . . .

. . . .

. . . .

. . . .

. . . .

. . . .

BOLD TRUST - Week 38
DEEPER TRUST

Cynthia

The SUV slid from side to side on the mud-slick road. Five of us were traveling as a team in Cambodia on a short-term mission We wereand on our way to visit a family who manufactured silk by hand in a remote village outside of Phnom Penh. The rain was torrential and the red dirt road seemed as if it would wash away at any moment. I was anxious and afraid that we wouldn't be able to make it back to the safety of our apartment in the city. At one point we thought we should turn around, but the majority ruled to keep on. Guess who the dissenting vote was? Yours truly.

When we finally arrived, we found the family hovering underneath their house, a ramshackle building seemingly in the middle of nowhere, trying to keep dry. They worked together in this house on crude stilts to make silk cloth to sell at the market several miles away. No electricity, no bathrooms, and no modern conveniences we are so accustomed to.

I tried really hard to pull out my trust badge, but I was shocked. It was so far from anything I had ever experienced, it paralyzed me in the moment. I am embarrassed to say I froze and couldn't wait to get back in the car and back to the city. I was completely out of my comfort zone and I didn't trust the situation or God.

A lack of trust can do that to a person. It can rattle your cage and tests the limits of your comfort zone. On a scale from one to hundred my discomfort zone was off the charts.

Later than night, when I was back in the safety of our little apartment in the city, I realized how deeply my trust had been challenged. I felt ashamed my faith was so weak that I couldn't trust God in the experience he presented that day. I allowed my anxiety and fear to dictate my trust level. I missed a God encounter with people who needed my compassion and love. Thankfully, the team I was with was much more experienced. Hopefully, this precious family didn't notice the wild-eyed stranger who couldn't wait to leave.

I concluded I didn't know God as well as I thought I did and confessed to him I needed his help to trust him deeper. Psalm 9:10 (NLT) says, "Those who know your name trust in you, for you, O Lord, do not abandon those who search for you."

The more we learn to know God, the more you and I can trust him. He is trustworthy no matter how far out of our comfort zone we find ourselves.

 BOLD ACTION STEP

Think about the last time you were out of your comfort zone. On a scale of one to ten, where was your trust level? What can you do differently next time? Spend some extra time this week getting to know God better so you can learn to trust him deeper.

VERSE OF THE WEEK

Those who know your name trust in you, for you, O Lord, do not abandon those who search for you.

(Ps. 9:10 NLT)

MY BOLD THOUGHTS

· ·

· ·

· ·

· ·

· ·

· ·

· ·

· ·

· ·

· ·

· ·

BOLD TRUST - Week 39
STRUGGLING TRUST

Andrea

Three years ago, God revealed to me that one day I would have a platform. The book promise was still lingering somewhere in the background, as my story hadn't even been written yet. I had no idea what having a platform meant, until the opportunity to write this book came along.

I have learned over the past few years miracles happen each time I step out of my comfort zone and trust, even when, humanly, it looks as if there is no way.

After two years of thinking it over, I finally gained the courage to leave the business my husband Dino and I started twenty years earlier. Running a business is what I did, but I knew it wasn't what I was called to do. I knew God had another chapter for me, but he was waiting for me to fully trust him.

When was the last time you stepped out and trusted God with everything? Would you still trust him if not everyone agrees with your bold steps of trust?

Where are you falling short in the trust department?

- Are you struggling with financial issues?
- Maybe you're the one struggling with your marriage today and you feel as if walking away is the only answer?
- Or are you the one afraid to take a step into sobriety because you've failed so many times before?

Closeness to God is not a feeling. Rather it's making a choice to obey our heavenly Father with everything he's instructed us to do. Trusting his instruction and the gifts he has entrusted us with, results in actions that are sure to bring him glory. Friends, our actions always follow our beliefs. If we believe in defeat that is what we will get. God already knows what he can do for us. He's looking for a tribe of warriors who trust him and step out boldly.

 BOLD ACTION STEP

What promise has God put in your heart? What steps do you need to take to bring this promise to fruition?

 VERSE OF THE WEEK

But blessed is the one who trusts in the Lord, whose confidence is in him. They will be like a tree planted by the water that sends out its roots by the stream. It does not fear when heat comes; its leaves are always green. It has no worries in a year of drought and never fails to bear fruit.

(Jer. 17:7–8 NIV)

⚓ MY BOLD THOUGHTS

. . . .

. . . .

. . . .

. . . .

. . . .

. . . .

. . . .

. . . .

. . . .

. . . .

. . . .

CHAPTER TEN

Bold Truth

INTRODUCTION
BIBLICAL TRUTH

Cynthia

HAVE YOU NOTICED HOW truth has "morphed" into whatever you feel *your* truth is? This has certainly crept into Christianity. Many professing Christians are getting sucked into the vortex of defining their own truth.

Now we will always have people who will question the truth of what we believe. It is good to examine and investigate to find the real truth. After all, if we were to all tell our stories, we were on our own journeys of searching for truth when we came to Christ. Christianity has been on the hot seat in all centuries, that's nothing new.

Recently I've sensed a greater cause for alarm because we seem to be moving farther and farther away from the "real truth" found in God's Word.

Chuck Colson writes in his book, *The Faith*, "Most Christians do not understand what they believe, why they believe it, and why it matters. How can a Christianity that is not understood by practiced?"

If we are to live out bold truth, we need to not only say we believe, but know why we believe it, and why it matters. We can't afford to be ignorant and assume people will understand what we are talking about when we explain the gospel.

As we explore bold truth this month in our devotional, ask God to show you the areas of your faith that need bolstering, so you can understand biblical truth, and how to live it out boldly.

BOLD TRUTH - Week 40
CHECKING IN

Andrea

A comfort zone. It's a cozy place, isn't it? The walls are filled with wooden picture frames with the words like "No Worries," "Be Happy," or "Hakuna Matata," the Swahili saying made famous in popular culture by the song from the movie *The Lion King*.

Your comfort zone is a safe place; so safe that you get comfortable there. Over time it feels like home. Your bags are unpacked, clothes folded nicely in the cedar dresser drawers. You've taken all your toiletries out of your bag and your favorite heels are lined up along the closet floor. You have "checked in" to the Comfort Zone Hotel.

We've all checked in one time or another. But, how often and how long we stay, is a choice.

For me, the longer I stayed isolated in my Comfort Zone Hotel room, ordering room service each morning instead of walking down to the lobby to eat breakfast, the more I felt stuck. I was stuck in a rut, a pit, a funk. As you read this, your own word may come to mind confirming you that you also have "checked in."

As sure as the sun will rise, one day you'll wake up and realize your quick weekend getaway has turned into an extended stay. Instead of hearing "Hakuna Matata" in your head and singing the *Lion King* song, you're rocking out and screaming the words to "Sweet Home Alabama."

Listen, friend, your life will have so much more meaning when you start living outside your comfort zone.

When I was growing up my dad would tell us: "If you always do what you've always done, you'll always get what you've always gotten." Later in life, when I was struggling to step out of my comfort zone, his words would replay in my head. Outside our comfort zones is where the unthinkable, the unimaginable, the impossible can happen.

 BOLD ACTION STEP

I encourage you this week to step outside your comfort zone. Write about the last time you did something for the first time. Rise up and do something this week your future self will thank you for.

 VERSE OF THE WEEK

But they who wait for the Lord shall renew their strength; they shall mount up with wings like eagles; they shall run and not be weary; they shall walk and not faint.

(Isa. 40:31 ESV)

MY BOLD THOUGHTS

....

....

....

....

....

....

....

....

....

....

....

....

BOLD TRUTH - Week 41
SPEAK TRUTH

Cynthia

I was in the kitchen one day when I heard a little voice say, "You are so good. She believes everything you say." I turned around to see my precious four-year-old boy looking at himself in the mirror of our armoire cabinet and congratulating himself for not telling me the truth earlier. I let him continue with his self-pep-talk for about five minutes. Finally, when I'd had quite enough, I interrupted him and spent the next several minutes as a teaching moment to talk about honesty and being truthful.

I don't think children are the only ones who struggle with being truthful. Adults wrestle with telling the truth, and with something deeper—being truthful with ourselves. Telling ourselves the truth is some of the hardest, deeper heart-work we will ever undertake. Our enemy, shame, robs us from admitting the truth. Shame speaks when we are afraid to tell ourselves the truth. If we do, shame says, "You are a bad person." Shame lies to us to keep us in the dark.

When we run from speaking truth to our hearts, we can fall into the trap of going from shame to blame to make ourselves feel better.

Have you ever believed the twisted lie that tells us, "You have failed," when you tell yourself the truth? God says differently. He promises to give us wisdom in the hidden places of our hearts. The Psalmist says, "Behold, you desire truth in the innermost being, and in the hidden part [of my heart] You will make me know wisdom" (Ps. 51:6 AMP). David wrote this psalm after he was confronted with his sin with Bathsheba (2 Sam. 12).

Wisdom is the payoff for telling ourselves the truth, admitting our weaknesses, owning up to our mistakes, recognizing our limits.

Next time you are afraid to tell yourself the truth about something, remember wisdom is around the corner. The truth will defeat the sinister enemy of shame and your heart will "know wisdom" in ways you've never experienced before.

➤ BOLD ACTION STEP

Spend some time this week answering these questions and filling in the blanks. Am I hiding anything? _____ What am I afraid to tell myself the truth about_____? I am blaming _____about_____. Then spend some time in prayer telling God the truth and ask him to give you a heart of wisdom in exchange for telling yourself the truth.

♡ VERSE OF THE WEEK

Behold, You desire truth in the innermost being, and in the hidden part [of my heart] You will make me know wisdom.

(Ps. 51:6 AMP)

MY BOLD THOUGHTS

BOLD TRUTH - Week 42
STRENGTH IN TRUTH

Andrea

Strong people go on, even when they think they can't. Strong people know God sees their sadness and their suffering. Strong people hand over everything to God in the hardest of times. Strong people know there's always a lesson in every pain or sorrow. Strong people know God is always good. Strong people know they can't succeed alone. Strong people pray for those in need. Strong people sacrifice themselves for others. Strong people know how to let others shine while standing in the spotlight. Strong people know forgiveness means giving up their right to hurt someone for hurting them. Strong people know it's OK to cry. Strong people know change is always coming and they're ready.

Strong people know the Bible is a road map for life. Strong people know family is the strongest bond they will ever have. Strong people love their children, but know their spouses come first. Strong people love their spouses but know God comes first.

Strong people understand life is a gift, and they treat it as such. Strong people know when they wake up each morning, the devil says, "Oh no, they're up." Strong people know when to say, no. Strong people know if they want something badly enough they will work hard to get it. Strong people are happy with other's successes, even if they don't experience success themselves.

Strong people act, they don't react. Strong people have a voice and they know when to use it. Strong people have a voice and know when *not* to use it. Strong people love deeply. Strong people care. Strong people know it takes courage to tell the truth, and also to sit and listen.

Strong people know they were created to worship God. Strong people are happy people. Strong people know the difference between "Will you please forgive me: I was wrong" and "Sorry!" Strong people tackle the unthinkable and give God the glory for when they get there. Strong people give their very best because they know God is watching.

Strong people have empathy. Strong people suffer and still serve. Strong people know we need darkness to see the stars. Strong people fight for the future God intended. Strong people know wisdom and knowledge mean nothing if kept a secret. Strong people share the truth with others and teach them how to be strong.

 BOLD ACTION STEP

What are your strengths? Write a paragraph or two about your strengths and ask God to help you use them for his glory this week.

♡ VERSE OF THE WEEK

God's name is a place of protection—good people can run there and be safe.

(Prov. 18:10 MSG)

MY BOLD THOUGHTS

BOLD TRUTH - Week 43
CHOOSE TRUTH

Andrea

"Will the *REALreal* Andrea please stand up?"

The problem was, no one stood.

I've spent most of my life trying to find out who I am. I've worn so many hats, over time, I struggled to know the real me.

When I finally stopped chasing who I was and understood the importance of *whose* I was, that's when I found the truth.

I have an inheritance in heaven unlike nothing here on earth. Because I know whose I am, I know my Father in heaven loves me despite my failures and shortcomings. If I were the only person on earth, he would have still sent his one and only Son to save me.

Others will never validate who I am. But whose am I am, you ask? I am a daughter of a King!

When God exposes the truth, it's another way he has to show us who he is. Don't be fooled. The things we keep hidden away under lock and key eventually will come out. When people see justice in your life, they won't see you; they'll see Jesus.

The truth can hurt, but it will set you free. If I had to make a choice to be hurt or be free, I would choose freedom every time.

Know this, when we choose truth, the enemy won't stop us from starting, he wants to stop us from finishing. He will stop at nothing to prevent you from seeing the truth. He'll whisper lies and tell you it's OK to blame the other person because you did nothing wrong. He tries to make you fearful by telling you all the horrible things that will happen if you tell the truth. Lies! If God has put something on your heart that needs to be exposed, it's because he wants you to walk in freedom. Have you heard the saying, "If God leads you to it, he'll see you through it"?

That my friends, is the real deal! Don't believe the lies.

 BOLD ACTION STEP

Do you want to experience freedom? Spend time with God this week and ask him to expose the truth. What do you need to do to be free? Write down the steps you will take to make it happen.

 VERSE OF THE WEEK

So Jesus said to the Jews who had believed him, "If you abide in my word, you are truly my disciples, and you will know the truth, and the truth will set you free."

(John 8:31–32 ESV)

⚓ MY BOLD THOUGHTS

. . . .

. . . .

. . . .

. . . .

. . . .

. . . .

. . . .

. . . .

. . . .

. . . .

. . . .

. . . .

BOLD TRUTH - Week 44
DECIDE TO BELIEVE

Andrea

Your pain, no matter the size or intensity, has purpose. Perhaps it's for you, someone you know, or someone who's watching. God wouldn't have allowed it if good was not going to be birthed from it.

Why? Because God is trustworthy!

Do you feel as if no one understands what you're going through this week? If you are reading this and experiencing a deep-seated pain, it may not seem like it right now . . . but Jesus understands.

Do you know that Jesus has experienced every emotion you have? Who better to trust with your heart than him?

During seasons in my life, I've held onto this verse, and I'd like to share it with you. "And we know that all things work together for good to those who love God, to those who are called according to *His* purpose" (Rom. 8:28 NKJV).

God's promise reads, "God, your God, will restore everything you lost; he'll have compassion on you; he'll come back and pick of the pieces from all the places where you were scattered" (Deut. 30:3 MSG).

Do you believe that "your God, will restore everything you lost."? It's a simple question. We all must choose whether we will believe what God's Word says. God loves us enough to allow me to make that choice for myself.

You see, we believe before we receive. We need to have trust and believe that God will make all things right, according to his will.

BOLD ACTION STEP

Think of the pieces of your heart that lie scattered along your journey. Name them. Thank God in advance for work he is doing in your life. Thank him now for the pieces he has picked up in the past and for the ones he will gather in the future.

 VERSE OF THE WEEK

God, your God, will restore everything you lost; he'll have compassion on you; he'll come back and pick of the pieces from all the places where you were scattered.

(Deut. 30:3 MSG)

MY BOLD THOUGHTS

CHAPTER ELEVEN

Bold Gratitude

INTRODUCTION
IT'S OVERWHELMING!

Andrea

OVERWHELMED. WE USUALLY GET there by Wednesday of each week, don't we? This week, let's look at the word overwhelmed from a different perspective.

Have you ever been extremely grateful for something God has given you . . . perhaps about an answered prayer for a loved one?

When I think of gratitude, I think of the world overwhelmed. God's goodness can be overwhelming.

It's so easy to move our eyes toward the things going wrong in our lives, we forget to be mindful of all the good things he's given to us.

In my life I have been in awe many times how God worked out a situation, or brought someone into my life at just the right time, or opened a door no man could shut. "The words of the holy one, the true one . . . who opens and no one will shut, who shuts and no one opens" (Rev. 3:7 ESV).

When we understand that God is able to give us everything we need, we feel an overwhelming sense of gratitude. "Now to him who is able to do far more abundantly than all that we ask or think, according to the power at work within us" (Eph. 3:20 ESV).

The next time someone asks you how you are doing, and you respond with, "I'm overwhelmed," remember you can be overwhelmed with thanksgiving and gratitude too!

BOLD GRATITUDE - Week 45
HIDDEN TREASURES

Cynthia

I lost a favorite earring one summer—my "go to" earrings for jeans-and-casual days. A few weeks later, I was digging around in the dirt in my front yard and spotted something silver, glimmering, and shiny. It was the earring I had lost. I have absolutely no idea how it landed in the dirt by my front walk. It's unexplainable.

I did a happy dance with dirt flying from my gardening gloves. I said, "Thank you!" loud enough for the whole neighborhood to hear and I didn't care. It was a gift from God, my treasure in the dirt that day.

Digging around in the dirt is cathartic for me. My heart was burdened that day with all the chaos in the world and some of my own challenges. I decided I needed to get down and dirty and replace my raggedy summer petunias with some decorative kale. When my hands are dirty and my head is bowing low to the ground planting, weeding, and digging, I can hear God whisper sweet words of calm to my heart.

Maybe it's the sense of the tangible, as I'm touching creation and watching with wonder how a seed turns into beauty. Or finding a bird's nest intricately constructed in one of my front pots. Nevertheless, I hear God in my garden and it makes my heart sing with gratitude.

Isaiah 45:3 reminds me that in all parts of life God will give me hidden treasures as I seek him. I wasn't expecting anything the day I found my earring. God gave me a little surprise to hold onto in the midst of my chaotic heart. He reminded me he's got this. I needed this desperately and am incredibly grateful God loves me enough to tangibly show me with the little things.

 BOLD ACTION STEP

So often we miss the opportunity to exercise gratitude. Think about the last few days and where can you find your own "treasure in the dirt." Write it on a 3 x 5 card and put it where you can see it for a week adding to the list. Tell God thank you for the small treasures and acts of love he presents every day.

 VERSE OF THE WEEK

I will give you hidden treasures, riches stored in secret places, so that you may know that I am the Lord, the God of Israel, who summons you by name.

(Isa. 45:3 NIV)

MY BOLD THOUGHTS

. . . .

. . . .

. . . .

. . . .

. . . .

. . . .

. . . .

. . . .

. . . .

. . . .

. . . .

BOLD GRATITUDE - **Week 46**
IN DARK MOMENTS

Andrea

I am grateful for my struggle. I know that sounds crazy, but it's true. Sometimes we find God in our most painful and darkest moments. How we handle the pain and disappointment of the things that have happened to us may be our greatest opportunity for a testimony. How we behave is not only a test of our character, but it can open the door to life-changing conversations. People are always watching.

During a year-long separation from my husband, God used the time to chisel away my character defects. He knew I couldn't carry those things where he was calling me to go. Dino and I worked hard on our relationship and God reconciled our marriage. Today, we both desire to be who God called us to be.

I never thought finding God again in the middle of my separation would be the most important part of my journey. Instead of just labeling myself as a Christian, today Jesus Christ is my Savior and Lord over my entire life. There's a big difference between the two.

The way we navigate through painful circumstances can leave lasting impressions on those around us. I am honored that God would choose ordinary me to impact someone else's future. There is peace in knowing God has used me to be his hands and feet.

You, dear friend, have the same opportunity as I had. Now *arise*! Go show the world there is hope.

BOLD ACTION STEP

Write down one of your greatest pains or darkest moments. How has God used this for good in your life? What did he reveal to you? If you don't have an answer, ask him to show you. It's there.

 VERSE OF THE WEEK

Don't fret or worry. Instead of worrying, pray. Let petitions and praises shape your worries into prayers, letting God know your concerns. Before you know it, a sense of God's wholeness, everything coming together for good, will come and settle you down. It's wonderful what happens when Christ displaces worry at the center of your life.

(Phil. 4:6–7 MSG)

MY BOLD THOUGHTS

BOLD GRATITUDE - Week 47
OUT OF THE HAZE

Cynthia

The sky looks like something out of an apocalyptic movie scene. There is a smoky haze suffocating the sun and blocking the normally beautiful blue sky of summer. We have been in a record heat wave and multiple wildfires are burning causing the smoke to drift miles from the fire. The air is thick and it's difficult to breathe.

Colors change under the haze and my flowerpots appear more brilliant. How odd that the sun's rays are diminished yet the vibrancy of color is so intense on my front porch.

The smoke and the haze serve as a reminder of how my heart can feel when it is overwhelmed and choked with sadness that the enemy uses to steal my joy.

Sometimes life just seems complicated and difficult. It doesn't always have to be the big crisis or the catastrophic events that can create a hazy smoke over my heart. Sometimes it is just a conglomeration of lots of little things that build into a crescendo of discouragement.

This is the remedy I find helpful for me when I am in a melancholy funk. I walk around my house and speak out loud as many things as I can think of to be thankful for. It does the trick! Gratitude lifts the gloomy haze over my heart.

Getting my mind out of the rut of the melancholy "sky-is-falling" mentality and focusing on being content and practicing joy isn't always easy, but it is necessary. In 1 Thessalonians 5:16–18 I am reminded to "Always be joyful, never stop praying, be thankful in all circumstances." To be honest, I don't like these verses, as *always* being joyful seems an impossible task. Yet when I kick my feelings out of the way and lean on the truth, something shifts first in my heart, and then in my emotions. In time, joy sets in. Even when the staggering little negatives pile up, I can choose joy by practicing being thankful.

 BOLD ACTION STEP

How about you, is there a bunch of little things that are attempting to make a pile and take away your joy? Determine to not let the haze cover up all the great things that can give you the vibrant color of joy in your lives!

 VERSE OF THE WEEK

Always be joyful. Never stop praying. Be thankful in all circumstances, for this is God's will for you who belong to Christ Jesus.

(1 Thess. 5:16–18 NLT)

⚓ MY BOLD THOUGHTS

BOLD GRATITUDE - Week 48
NO MORE EXCUSES

Andrea

There comes a time in every girl's life when she says, "Enough!" No more procrastinating, no more excuses!

God nudged my heart this morning at 6:30 a.m. He impressed an invitation upon my heart, *Spend some time with me this morning . . . outside.*

I knew it would take some fortitude to peel myself away from my warm, cozy bed. Those who know me well know I'm not a morning person. I typically get my second wind at 11 p.m. But I got up and dressed to go out, tying a light scarf around my neck. It was cold outside but I debated bringing it because I knew once I started walking, I wouldn't need it. But for some reason, I took it anyway.

As I walked, I reflected on a conversation I had with my husband the night before. I told him about the journey I'd started to get healthier. I wanted to make sure I would be around to live a long life with him and for kids and grandkids. But the bigger reason for getting healthier was because of the things God had put on my heart recently. I kept hearing, *Andrea, I can't use you if you are not healthy, and I certainly can't use you if you are not here.* So, I made a vow to use this body I've been given and to treat it with respect. Every day.

It was still early. The sun was out but it had not crested the top of the hills. As I walked around the high school track, I looked up at the hills as the sun poked its head up. Looking at the beauty of the sunrise, I was overwhelmed with gratitude. God woke me up early on a Sunday morning because he had something beautiful he wanted to show me.

And the scarf I didn't think I'd need? I used it to blow my nose and wipe my face as tears of gratitude rolled down my cheeks.

There is joy in the morning when we choose to believe God has the "already" to every circumstance, and every "what if?"

God loves you too much to leave you where you are. He sees such great potential in you. Be grateful for where you are and have hope for your future. He wants you to flourish. So, rejoice in knowing something beautiful is on the horizon.

 **BOLD ACTION STEP**

In your journal, write about an area in your life where you need to be healthier or need to make a change. Ask God for a first step to take to start this journey.

♡ VERSE OF THE WEEK

My counsel for you is simple and straightforward: Just go ahead with what you've been given. You received Christ Jesus, the Master; now *live* him. You're deeply rooted in him. You're well constructed upon him. You know your way around the faith. Now do what you've been taught. School's out; quit studying the subject and start *living* it! And let your living spill over into thanksgiving.

(Col. 2:6–7 MSG)

⚓ MY BOLD THOUGHTS

. . . .

. . . .

. . . .

. . . .

. . . .

. . . .

. . . .

. . . .

. . . .

. . . .

. . . .

. . . .

CHAPTER TWELVE

Bold Stories

INTRODUCTION
TELL YOUR STORY

Andrea

OUR STORIES ARE POWERFUL and are opportunities for God to show us just how big he is!

For some, this may be the hardest chapter in this book. It can be intimidating to use our voices and share our stories. It means being transparent and vulnerable. Do you know God deeply cares about our stories? He intentionally weaves together relationships that become stories. If we are unwilling to share, someone may miss the blessing of hearing your story.

Many of you want to be bold storytellers, but are afraid because revealing yourself may change the way people perceive you. Let God worry about that! He can change hearts and cause people to see you the way he wants them to. I'm not encouraging you to disregard the feelings or opinions of others, but remember, feelings and opinions are just feelings and opinions.

You live for an audience of One; it is only him you will stand before one day. If God is nudging you to share your story, get ready! He may already have someone in mind who desperately needs to hear your story. All you have to do is say, "Yes!"

"Great is our Lord and mighty in power; his understanding has no limit" (Ps. 147:5 NIV).

BOLD STORIES - Week 49
WHO'S WRITING THIS STORY ANYWAY?

Cynthia

Have you ever thought of your life as being a story? A book? Maybe a novel?

God is in fact writing our stories. He is the author of our lives—if we partner together with him to let him write it.

The writer of Hebrews says, "Looking unto Jesus the author and perfecter of our faith" (Heb. 12:2 ASV). God will finish what he has started in our lives.

> There has never been the slightest doubt in my mind that the God who started this great work in you would keep at it and bring it to a flourishing finish on the very day Christ Jesus appears.
>
> (Phil. 1:6 MSG)

These aren't just warm fuzzy words but concrete promises telling us the God who created us has a plan. He doesn't leave us as a lump of useless clay. He is purposeful. He is perfecting us and is writing each word from the start of our first breath until we take our last.

I don't know about you but that gives me hope. I can relax because I can trust that everything in life that comes knocking on my door is a part of my story. I can hold onto the promise that God will bring me to a flourishing finish.

There is one caveat.

I need to acknowledge his work in my life and trust him with the outcome even when I don't know how it will end. That means I have to relinquish control. Ouch! If I trust God to be the author of my story, I need to come alongside and release my will and my way. Easier said than done, right?

It's a bold step to allow God to write our stories. I've come to learn that he does a much better job of perfecting my faith than me. The key is to allow him and embrace the process.

For the author, writing is a process; it takes time. Each word that gets put on a page comes as a result of letting go and trusting the process.

It is the same with acknowledging God as the author of your story and mine. It is a process. We have to embrace. Trust. Surrender. Let go.

 BOLD ACTION STEP

Which part of your story have you been resisting lately? On a sheet of paper, create a storyboard of significant events in your life, both the highs and the lows. Keep it with your *Live Bold Journal* and thank God for writing your story.

VERSE OF THE WEEK

And I am sure of this, that he who began a good work in you will bring it to completion at the day of Jesus Christ.

(Phil. 1:6 ESV)

MY BOLD THOUGHTS

BOLD STORIES - Week 50
SHARE YOUR STORY

Andrea

In 1912, Niles, California was home to one of the first motion picture companies on the West Coast. Charlie Chaplin and Bronco Billy Anderson filmed some of their now famous silent movies in downtown Niles.

One afternoon in downtown Niles, I stopped by a charming tearoom that offers a Victorian tea experience. As I sipped a hot cup of English black tea from a china teacup, I looked up as a trio walked in. I pulled out my notebook to describe what I saw:

They caught my eye, two young girls, sitting at the table next to me. Their faces told the story of feeling so grown, while sipping on afternoon tea.

Croissants and sandwiches with jellies and jams lined their china plate. Their giggles and smiles brightened the room, with each tiny bite they ate.

The stares were present around the room; you could hear the gossip and talk.
A whisper here and a whisper there of what the girls had brought.

He could feel it too as he sat there, he acted like it wasn't a bother.
He carried himself like the proud one; after all he was their father.

"How cute. Are these your daughters?" A lady walked up to say.
But the answer the father gave, inspired my writing today.

"I'm teaching them how to be a lady." His words sunk deep in my heart. It was clear what I needed to write about, I knew exactly where to start.

He was not concerned with how he looked in this tearoom today. What mattered the most were his daughters, how being their daddy was portrayed.

A tea party back at home, no one would ever have known. But he chose to have it in public; the true love of a father was shown.

I hope his girls will remember, how their father went out of his way. To make sure they knew they were special, because we all saw it today.

I felt a familiar nudge, and walked over to their table. Introducing myself as a writer, I said, "I have written a poem for you." After handing him my card, I asked for, and received, his permission to post this story on my blog.

Four years later at a graduation party, this stranger and I crossed paths again.

He noticed me as I walked in and whispered to his wife, "Hey, that's the lady who wrote the blog about the girls and me." He walked over and told me he was inspired to live a more intentional life after reading my blog. Today, that poem hangs in his room as a reminder, a gift from his wife on his birthday.

Sharing our stories doesn't necessarily need to be only about us. The next time you're in a restaurant and see a mom with three small children trying to hold it together, tell her what a great job she's doing. Or if you notice a grandfather teaching his grandson how to build something, comment.

Have you considered maybe God wants you to say something when thoughts come to your mind?

The man I wrote the poem about later told me, "That boldness forever changed what I thought being bold was." Remarkably, this story continues. Together we created a movement in our community, called Be Bold, Speak Truth, encouraging others to share their stories. (If you are interested in starting one in your community, please refer to the contact information in the back of this book.)

➤ BOLD ACTION STEP

Your mission this week is to find two people (preferably strangers) you can speak truth into. Journal what you observed and what you said. Then document their response. Continue this in your own family, by having weekly challenges to do so. We can give our children and grandchildren the tools to help change the future.

♡ VERSE OF THE WEEK

But how can people call for help if they don't know who to trust? And how can they know who to trust if they haven't heard of the One who can be trusted? And how can they hear if nobody tells them? And how is anyone going to tell them, unless someone is sent to do it?

(Rom. 10:14 MSG)

MY BOLD THOUGHTS

BOLD STORIES - Week 51
THE GREATEST STORY EVER TOLD

Cynthia

In one of the boldest stories in the Bible, the characters are many but each person has a specific role to play. It is the story of how God orchestrated the miracle of bringing reconciliation to His creation. The characters are unforgettable:

Gabriel and Mary

Mary and Joseph

The innkeeper and the animals

The shepherds and the angels

The brilliant star and the wisemen

Jesus in the manger

It's the greatest story ever told, enduring for centuries, marking hope for eternity. We read the story every year in Luke 2 and sing carols. We watch adorable children in Sunday school act out the story. We send cards with nativity scenes and messages of joy.

The story.

It's timeless and yet it's easy to forget it is more than a story we replicate with our decorative nativity scenes. It is the central message of the gospel.

Jesus, the greatest storyteller, is both the author and the main character in sacrificial redemption for you and for me. Without his story, there would be no God story in each of us.

Jesus gives us reason to continue to allow the author of the universe to write our stories. There is always hope; there is always a victory chapter around the corner. Because of the first story that was written for you and me we can sing, "O come let us adore Him, Christ the Lord."

And yet, Christmas still tempts all kinds of emotions. It can trigger events we'd like to forget and people we'd rather not remember. The imperfect story of Christmas can be the antidote for those triggers. Can we choose to rejoice in Christmas and in the story God is writing on our hearts despite the things we want to ignore?

It's possible because of the miracle in the manger. We just have to be bold enough and choose to allow God to write our story with all the imperfect pieces.

The Christmas story is messy from beginning to end. It is stressful from the moment the angel Gabriel visited Mary to the unlikely place of finding Jesus on a bed of straw in a barn. And yet the angels sang and the shepherds worshipped.

 BOLD ACTION STEP

Make a list of the imperfect pieces in your life that you might be trying to ignore. Place your list in an envelope and put it under the tree as a gift to Jesus and a reminder that God is writing your story. When Christmas comes find a quiet place and offer it to him as an act of worship and thank him for both the hard and joyful places in your life.

 VERSE OF THE WEEK

Come and listen, all you who fear God, and I will tell you what he did for me.

(Ps. 66:16 NLT)

MY BOLD THOUGHTS

· ·

· ·

· ·

· ·

· ·

· ·

· ·

· ·

· ·

· ·

· ·

· ·

BOLD STORIES - Week 52
CRAFT YOUR STORY

Cynthia

We want you to have an opportunity this last week to craft your story. You've read our stories the past fifty-one weeks. They've encouraged you to walk boldly and live out God's truth in your own life.

Now it's your turn to be bold and tell your story.

Your Bold Action Step this week is to take some time to write a part of your story. You might not know exactly where to begin, so here's our suggestion: pray and then write!

One way to begin is to list significant people, events, and places that have had an impact in your life. Use bullet points and short phrases for each one. Organize your list and then start writing. Choose a few ideas and think of it as if you are writing a chapter for each event. Focus on how the people, event, or place motivated you to grow, change, and be bold.

You might not be a writer, but you are the best person to tell your story! Don't pass up this last Bold Action Step.

We invite you to share your story with us at www.livingbold.org to encourage others to live bold and leave a legacy!

MY STORY

. . . .

. . . .

. . . .

. . . .

. . . .

. . . .

. . . .

. . . .

. . . .

. . . .

. . . .

. . . .

MY STORY

Scripture Index

Psalm 107:8–9
Love: Week 15

Jeremiah 32:27
Obedience: Week 8

Proverbs 18:10
Truth: Week 42

Daniel 4:2
Tell Your Story: Week 52

Proverbs 18:24
Friendship: Week 34

Matthew 18:20
Prayer: Week 18

Proverbs 27:17
Friendship: Week 32

Luke 1:45
Faith: Week 3

Isaiah 30:15
Trust: Week 36

John 1:12
Identity: Week 12

Isaiah 40:11
Identity: Week 11

John 8:31–32
Truth: Week 43

Isaiah 40:31
Truth: Week 40

Romans 10:14
Tell Your Story: Week 50

Isaiah 45:3
Gratitude: Week 45

Romans 14:13
Compassion: Week 24

Jeremiah 17:7–8
Trust: Week 39

1 Corinthians 15:58
Prayer: Week 22

Jeremiah 29:11
Obedience: Week 7

I Corinthians 16:13–14
Love: Week 16

James 4:8–10
Faith: Week 5

2 Peter 1:3
Service: Week 31

Acknowledgments

Andrea

THANK YOU TO REDEMPTION Press for believing in this idea and helping us turn it into something so incredible. Athena Dean Holtz, thank you for reminding me that my "suddenly" was coming.

To Inger Logelin who edited this book and brought her wisdom and gift of words. Thank you for helping us make something so extraordinary.

To my Tribe, you know who you are. There are so many of you, it would take pages to name you all. Thank you for believing in me.

To my husband Dino, thank you for understanding when I worked on this book at all hours of the night trying to finish. But more importantly, thank you for allowing me to walk away from the business we started together, to do the things God placed upon my heart. I love you for that.

To my children, Hammer (Laura), Kirsti (Nick), and Angelo, you inspire me to be better than I was yesterday. My grandchildren, you keep me young, and continue to teach me it's OK to be me, the real me.

Pastor Fred, you believed in me from day one, and have always encouraged me to follow my calling; thank you.

Bridges Community Church, thank you for being my home for the past thirty-eight years. Thank you for bringing the Celebrate Recovery program to our church where I have found freedom from my hurts, habits, and hang-ups. It transformed my life and saved my marriage and I am forever grateful.

My parents, thank you for the sacrifices you made for me growing up and for continuing the legacy of Christ in our family.

My sister, Corrine and my brother, Brent, thank you for walking this journey with me the past four years.

Cynthia, my cuz. Thank you for never making me feel inferior as a first-time author and for loving me the way you do. I appreciate the way you have held my hand through this whole process. I have learned from the very best!

And to my Lord and Savior Jesus Christ, thank you for these bold stories. Thank you for impressing a promise upon my heart that one day I would write a book. You continued to chase me until I finally gave in and gave you my whole heart. There's nothing I wouldn't do for you.

Cynthia

This is the first time I've had the honor of co-authoring a book. I want to thank Andrea, for trusting me to lead. Her tender insight and wisdom was inspiring as we wove the pieces together to create this devotional. It is truly a joy to work together, and even more meaningful because we are family. I love you cousin!

To my husband Kevin who continues to be my cheerleader on multiple book projects. Your flexibility on late nights and late meals, speaks love and support as I write. Thank you, you are the best!

To my family—the ever-growing Cavanaugh Clan, our children and grandchildren, thank you for believing in my dreams.

To my tribe, writer friends, and Diva Prayer Group, I love walking together on this writing journey to make a difference with our words. Your prayers give me the fuel to push ahead when I feel uncertain.

To the Redemption Press team who are committed to publish with integrity and excellence. Kate, our faithful, encouraging project manager, Inger our fabulous wordsmith editor, and to the design team. Thank you!

To Jesus my rock, Redeemer, and Savior who turned my messy life into a message bringing hope to others. He is teaching me I don't have to be perfect to live bold and leave a legacy that matters.

Contact Us

YOU CAN FIND ANDREA AT:

www.andreatomassi.com

CYNTHIA AT:

www.cynthiacavanaugh.com

OR YOU CAN LEARN MORE ABOUT LIVE BOLD AT:

www.livingbold.org

Order Information

REDEMPTION PRESS

To order additional copies of this book, please visit
www.redemption-press.com.
Also available on Amazon.com and BarnesandNoble.com
Or by calling toll free 1-844-2REDEEM.